L. F.

D1231749

WORDS OF FAITH

Nihil Obstat
    Rt. Rev. Thomas V. Cassidy
        Censor Librorum

Imprimatur
    ✠Russell J. McVinney, D.D.
        Bishop of Providence

July 30, 1955

WORDS OF FAITH

by

FRANÇOIS MAURIAC

PHILOSOPHICAL LIBRARY
NEW YORK

Copyright 1955 by Philosophical Library, Inc.
15 East 40th Street, New York 16, N. Y.
All rights reserved.

Translated from the original
French *Paroles Catholiques* by
REV. EDWARD H. FLANNERY

Printed in the United States of America
by The Haddon Craftsmen, Inc.

204
M454w

71318

Table of Contents

WORDS OF FAITH

I

*Spoken in Spain**

ONE of our greatest poets, Charles Baudelaire, once complained that in France everyone resembles Voltaire. It was a good jest and not, indeed, without its grain of truth. The flair for what is reasonable and clear, a loathing for the irrational, a distrust of whatever is not verifiable by reason: here is the pith of the Voltairean spirit and, to a certain degree, of the French spirit as well.

I say "to a certain degree" because the France of Rabelais, Montaigne, and Molière, the France of Voltaire and the Encyclopedists has always found itself pitted against the Christian France of Bossuet and Pascal.

What is the present state of this perennial debate, which with varying fortunes has gone on from generation to generation? How does it look to a Frenchman of today? I dare not tell you that this vast

* Text of a discourse delivered in Madrid in 1929.

1

question is going to be our subject this evening; just to pose it properly would alone take more than an hour.

My goal is much more modest. I wish simply to cast a glance about that corner of the great field of battle which destiny has made my home and to describe for you what I see there. "Field of battle," did I say? My words do violence to my thought. For in the literary climate disagreements of an intellectual or religious nature are far less likely to incite the hostility they would, for example, in politics. As often as not, our adversary turns out to be an instructor who enjoys our admiration as well as our respect, or a friend to whom we are tied by bonds of genuine affection. So I am confident that it will be an easy matter for me to keep this debate, which otherwise could be so fierce, above controversy and on a lofty and serene plane. As a matter of fact, in this debate your countryman, and my friend, Ramón Fernández, has displayed so much wisdom and restraint that I shall be forced to reply less to what he actually said than to what he merely implied.

But first I must apologize for asking you to meditate for an hour with me, when perhaps all you wished to do here was to relax. You are the victims, I am afraid, of a particular idea that I have always had

2

of Spain and of the Spanish. I began by citing the remark of one of our poets: "In France, everyone resembles Voltaire." Well, I have never been able to think of Spain without seeing the face of Theresa of Avila or the countenance of Saint John of the Cross. Despite the thousand and one features that Spain could exhibit to dazzle a Frenchman from Gascogny, it remains for me above all that spot on earth where man touched God at closest range, where the embrace of the Creator and the creature was more intimate than anywhere else in the world. The same daring which lured so many of your heroes toward uncharted seas and the Indies urged them also upward toward the Infinite Spirit, which they embraced. And just as your navigators traced our maps, so your mystics received the grace to mark off the paths which brought them to such heights. Among all the victories of which Spain could boast, the one which has always fascinated me is expressed in that superb statement of Theresa of Avila: "I was not quite twenty years old when I trod upon a vanquished world."

Then again, a Frenchman born in Bordeaux, a native of Landes, who spent his entire youth at your very gates is familiar with the other faces of Spain. The patois spoken around us in my youth was replete, enriched with words from Spanish. When a storm was brewing, we would ask if it came from Spain, just to know if it was going to be a bad one; and I remember how we used to close our eyes and dilate our nostrils upon feeling that Spanish wind on our little faces, a gust that at once enchanted our senses but burned our skins. And at college in Bordeaux, we used always to be on pins and needles when Vespers lagged for fear we might miss the first bull. We would hurry along the dusty road those summer Sundays keeping pace with the old Victorian phaetons that approached the arenas, their embroideries glistening in the sun—*Guerita* and *Reverte*, *Albeno* and *Mazzantini*.

But, in the end, it was by its heroism that this Spain, which I found so charming, captivated me. And if I have delighted in retracing on her roads the footsteps of Don Quixote and on the high seas the wake of Columbus' caravels, I have never felt that I was tasting her genius at its best except in those of her sons and daughters in whom heroism went beyond itself and was transformed into sanctity.

That is the reason why it occurred to me quite naturally to speak to you on a subject so close to my heart. If one of my own countrymen could say that in France everyone resembles Voltaire, how much more striking must this resemblance be to Spanish eyes! What probably impresses you in the France of today and surely must have impressed you as you listened to Ramón Fernández the other evening was, whether you like them or not, the qualities of good sense and reason, the taste for rational verification, the mistrust of (not to say a hostility toward) whatever is not reducible to clear-cut formulas, of whatever is not an object of experience: in short, a hatred of the mysterious and a denial of the supernatural.

And yet a French spirituality does exist. After so many dogged and violent assaults it has survived, though to all appearances repressed, impoverished, and defeated. Repressed, yet gathering force in the secret recesses of many souls; impoverished and seemingly defeated, yet gaining strength from its very weakness.

Of course, I cannot expect you to accept all this on my say-so alone. From my books or from what you may have heard about me, you know where my preferences lie; and you are probably saying already that I am preaching for my parish priest. You may say that a Catholic, with all the good faith in the world, tends to attach importance to questions which no longer interest anyone but himself and his friends.

However, I give you my word, I am at pains to put aside my own hopes and preferences. With all the objectivity I am capable of, I scan the ruins of French Catholicism.

Following an assault of more than two centuries, these ruins are vast; a mere glance is enough to confirm this. But what is also apparent is that the cause of this disaster is not to be found within Catholic doctrine itself but outside it, in historical and political happenings. This should be apparent even to our foes, if they are attentive to the facts and sincerely disposed. The manifold abuses, the privileged status of the Church in the *ancien régime,* to choose but one example, are at the root of much of the anti-clericalism in our provinces. Then at the turn of the century, certain laws, already well ripened from long preparation behind the scenes, were applied with patience and tenacity. These laws systematically destroyed almost every channel through which Christian metaphysics had reached our children, and particularly the children of the people.

The triumph of a certain theory of the all-powerful laicized State is what dealt the rudest blow to Christianity in France. (This conception, to be truthful, has never lacked its defenders in my country's history; we find them among the jurists of our Most Christian King as well as among the Jacobins of the

Convention.) Only the outer scaffolding, however, the organization and framework, was affected, not the doctrine. The living water could be diverted from those souls no longer partaking of it, but it was never itself to run dry or lose its purity. Christian dogma, momentarily dimmed by Scientism, shines forth today unimpaired. Just as Christ once passed in the midst of those who would stone him, only to elude them, as St. John shows us, so does He escape the thousand and one contradictory theories hurled at Him by the higher criticism; and He lives among us yet.

If Catholicism in France has suffered greatly from the alienation of the masses and the indifference or hostility of the State, perhaps it has reaped some advantages as well. First of all, in proportion as the Christian tide recedes from institutions and customs, it reaches new depths in souls. Yes, in my homeland Christianity gains in intensity what it loses in extension. Those who believe have a more vibrant faith, and those who love venture further in their love. It may be that a triumphant God is less loved than a forsaken one.

As the world returns to paganism, Christianity seems to revert to its source. Not only are faith and love renewed in faithful souls; but in the others the recoil from the Christian ideal leaves a void that defies every effort to fill it. Among the vast throngs left defenseless by the withdrawal of the Spirit, a certain lack, a deficiency is evident: a gaping hollow, a sense of infinite emptiness which smites the less resourceful. One common trait that links all the philosophical and literary extremes in vogue today —Surrealism, for instance—is the fact that they are mysticisms from which God is missing. It is these mysticisms without God that are at the root of our despair.

In an age of drugs and narcotics, I might add, despair is all about us; not even the well-fed bourgeoisie is spared. Every day the number of addicts to intoxicants and soporifics continues to grow. True, the group is still small. Never before, however, has Christ's affirmation that He is the Life held greater meaning. He *is* the life, literally—even for the body. For those who, having lost Him, seek escape in drunkenness and sleep, His absence is mortal.

To sleep is my one desire, to sleep rather than live . . .
In a slumber as sweet as death . . .

In these lines of Baudelaire we hear the troubled sigh of the great army of addicts, the sigh of those who in their self-made Paradise will not be consoled for their loss of the true Paradise.

Many of the learned will smile, no doubt, together with my friend Fernández, and suspect that I am seeing things in their darkest hue to suit my purpose. Many will assure me that they have not given themselves to any kind of excess, that their heads are solidly on their shoulders and their hearts firmly in place, and that they feel no need of a belief in a God to live reasonably or to strike a satisfactory balance of their instincts and their higher aspirations. They glory in the name of humanist in the strongest sense of the term. They are men, and nothing human is alien to them; but, on the other hand, whatever exceeds the human is, to say the least, suspect. They want nothing founded on sentiment, and they do not want sentiment encroaching on the realm of thought. Themselves alone they know with certitude; and in themselves alone, not in some unverifiable supernatural, do they intend to discover the elements of their personality.

And still, there is something in these humanists, these erudite adversaries of the Christian metaphysic, which impresses me. They no longer disregard the succor that mankind has found, and continues to find, in faith. Far, indeed, from treating religion with

9

disdain, they are at pains to capture its secret. Yes, assuredly, they admit of nothing in this wide world but the human and they disallow all that surpasses human experience; it is on the basis of self knowledge that they would mould their personal life. Nevertheless, they give serious consideration to the whole question of whether this sort of personal life will fill the place of religious living, and whether they will find within themselves the daily strength that the believer finds in his religious life.

Frenchmen like these, therefore, do not quite resemble Voltaire. To tell the truth, they resemble Voltaire a good deal less than they do Montaigne, whom Ramón Fernández has hailed as his master. Montaigne who in his *Essays,* makes of his life a laboratory for watching himself live, and whose only concern is to disfigure nothing within him; Montaigne, to whom the Christian idea of interior progress, of seeking perfection, is odious, and who, doting on himself, wills that he be just as he is. Here, in effect, is the real father of the humanists of today.

Yet, I repeat, equally hostile to Christian thought as Voltaire and his school, these humanists do not for all that share Voltaire's disdain for Christianity. Instead of thinking, as he did, that a religion for the people is needed, they are tempted rather to say that it is a religion for the elite that is necessary. It has not escaped their notice that Christianity has resolved that which for them ever remains the difficult problem: to organize the interior life after the pattern of an external and ever present model; to use, discard, and select, in accord with it, whatever in each being has the makings of a living person.

Like Taine and the rationalists of fifty years ago, our present-day humanists, you may be sure, do not admit that the Unknown Being can be proved or become an object of certitude. Even though they persist in thinking that believers create this God whom they adore wholly by projecting outward the values they find within themselves, at least they are no longer so assured of the collapse, either imminent or remote, of a religion which they observe attracting so many souls. Here again, they are far from Voltaire. For the Eighteenth Century philosophers and their heirs in the Twentieth were dominated by the idea that Christianity was virtually finished, and that the theological stage of mankind was over. They were convinced that in its forward march, the modern world was in the process of eliminating the ancient metaphysics, whose disappearance would be in direct ratio to the progress of science.

Our humanists of today are not so sure. This does

not mean that they have ceased exploiting the difficulties that historical science casts in the path of religion. It is simply that more than a century after the onset of the debate, the evidence seems conclusive that on this terrain nothing decisive will be unearthed against the Christ of History. The development and progress of the science of Exegesis constantly calls into question matters which had been deemed definitely settled. At present, independent criticism dealing with the historicity of the New Testament comes closer every day to what the Church has always taught. Catholic exegetes like Father de Grandmaison or Father Lagrange see their position reinforced by the discoveries of the illustrious Jesuit, Father Jousse, on the psychology of language and the oral transmission of the words of Christ. Actually, the exegetical difficulties raised against the Church, to my mind, carry little weight against the formidable fact with which she is able to confront her adversaries. This fact can be expressed in a single word: Christ: that Man, that sign of contradiction, who at a precise interval of time and space came to divide human history into two parts. It is now a certainty that no objection of a historical nature will prevail against Christianity's charm. The old religious chanson, which Jaurés used to poke fun at, once more assumes for discriminating minds the proportions of a great symphony, at once human and divine,—though, unhappily, it no longer soothes the souls of the masses.

A detestable charm it is, no doubt, in the eyes of the humanist. For, as he sees it, by providing in the person of Christ a visible model which man must imitate, and by forcing him to recognize the distinction between right and wrong as it has been fixed for all time, Christianity obligates him to sacrifice an essential part of his personality in the name of values that are out-of-date and no longer meet the requirements of modern life.

The humanist will not abide any violence to his ego; he accepts himself wholly as he is. "An honest man," said Montaigne, "is a mixed man." Christianity's dreadful defect, to the humanist's way of thinking is precisely its desire to iron out our undulant and multiform nature, on the pretext of uplifting him and raising him to the level of the imitation of Christ. This only diminishes and constricts him.

According to the humanist, we become Christians only by sacrificing what is most truly ourselves. He suggests, therefore, that we sacrifice nothing, that our design of living (a design which will one day, perchance, be a living picture for others to admire)

13

should include our virtues and our vices without moral preoccupations, or at least without any pre-occupations of traditional morality, by utilizing the best and the worst in us—that is, if we can speak in terms of best or worst. Everything is good; everything can help to create a heroic portrait; everything must be exposed to the risks of experience. It is in this context that André Gide admiringly quotes Montaigne's words: "There is no way of life so feeble as that ruled by order and discipline."

But if Christian man is so diminished, so poor and so meager, so compelled to follow outdated and outmoded precepts no longer attuned to the basic needs of his life, as the humanist says he is, how then is he able—solely by virtue of being a Christian, however humble—to behave in a manner so personal, so individual, and so original? Whence does this supposedly mutilated Christian derive his almost overdeveloped inner life? I am struck by the fact that the concept of personality professed by my friend Ramón Fernández is, by his own avowal, incapable of replacing Catholicism without itself assuming a religious character. He did not admit this to you the other evening, but he has written it. Once aware of our total resources, we must risk our all, he writes, "as if by the command of a God." That is what he says, but that

14

precisely is what can never be: God is not invented, nor created.

And it is here that we come upon the ineffable Christian mystery which at one stroke reduces to nought the humanist's claim that the imitation of Christ condemns us to a diminished and impoverished state, the mystery which unveils the secret of that burning personal life, and that ceaseless inner drama which gives Christian destiny its intensity. This uniform model, this unique Christ after whom we are accused of wanting to pattern every human being, is anything but a lifeless model, wholly external to us, whose features it is our job to copy as patiently and skillfully as possible. Indeed, it is less a matter of imitating or copying Him than of uniting ourselves to Him.

Union with Christ: the very phrase is the answer to the objection of the humanist. When St. Paul exclaims: "It is now no longer I that live, but Christ lives in me," it is obvious that none of the traits that characterized St. Paul's powerful personality were attenuated or destroyed, but, on the contrary, were infinitely strengthened. The Christ living in us possesses us totally and He, much more than the self-centered man, puts all to use; he changes water into wine, transmutes vices into virtues in those secret

15

nuptials of Cana performed in each of us. We are not dealing here with mere proverbs or dicta which together with the forces of heredity, habit, and education might help us to live fairly good lives; it is a living voice within, which in each individual case makes known what is required. Nothing, in fact, is less fixed, nothing less set or more personal than the life of a Christian. Yes, I realize this means that nothing is left to chance, that we know exactly where we are going. "Be ye perfect as your heavenly Father is perfect." This commandment is for everyone. It is a matter of our becoming saints.

This is true. However, if the direction is the same for all, the prodigious diversity among the saints whom the Church offers for our veneration is evidence of how well she has succeeded in coping with the problem of personality. In spite of the mystical bond uniting them, what a difference between St. Theresa and St. John of the Cross! And between the latter and St. Ignatius Loyola! Each and every Christian life is an original creation. The diversity of religious orders in itself bears witness to what degree the unique notion of the life of perfection comprises differences, contrasts, and nuances.

And let us not hesitate at this point to take the offensive. Let us dare to declare that Christ is the greatest Creator of personalities that this world has ever seen. These are words that come easily to one's lips in the presence of fellow-countrymen of Theresa and John of the Cross, of Peter Alcántara and Ignatius of Loyola. There can be no doubt. Christ living within us annexes every part of us; like a magnet which attracts metal filings and clasps each particle as in a close embrace, He draws, clasps, harmonizes, divinizes our instincts, our passions, our feelings and our thoughts. And from this multiplicity he refashions in his love that immortal unity, our soul.

The humanist also is concerned about this same problem of his own inner multiplicity. But he is anxious to solve it alone, and, without relinquishing any part of himself, to become someone, or in other words, to realize his possibilities. But at the very outset he runs into a trap from which the humanist rarely manages to escape. The desire to make himself over, he finds, is not nearly so compelling as the pleasure of watching and observing, of doting on self. "Everything about himself," writes André Gide of Montaigne, "is to him an object of curiosity, amusement, and surprise." And so, fascinated with the flux of his own states of consciousness, with the perpetual motion within, he fails at first to grasp that what so fascinates and amuses him is anything but an anodyne force. It takes some time to discover that this inner world which he wishes to gaze on without interfering is peopled with instincts to be feared. This young animal whose feline grace charms us is hard to imagine as the ferocious beast it is about to become; but before long its capers take a dangerous turn; its gnawing begins to pain, its claws draw blood, and the wounds become poisonous.

Meanwhile, we find that our complacency and our resolve not to interfere in almost every case favors our lower instincts, those forces which distinguish us least and depersonalize us most. Where shameful actions are concerned, the greatest philosopher is no better off than the scoundrel and the scamp. Which is the same as saying that he who hopes to save his personality, yet deny himself nothing, will lose it.

Aren't you claiming then, the humanist will say, that life can be fulfilled by cautiously testing and weighing every situation? Yes, for the materials on hand for the task are not purely passive and such as you can take or leave at will. The things we do most readily, the choices we feel most urgently compelled to make, are precisely those which the higher dictates of our conscience reject. "We do not understand ourselves," said St. Theresa of Avila, "we do not know what we want, and we go infinitely far away from what we desire." And echoing the word of your saint, a great Frenchman and Catholic, Maurice Blondel, exclaims: "Sometimes I do not do all that I want; at other times, almost without realizing it, I do what I do not want to do. And once these deeds are done, they weigh upon my entire life. I am, as it were, their prisoner."

Whatever you may say, that which you call your *self* is far from passive; you simply cannot make up your mind to ignore it, you cannot unleash or check those obscure forces as you would a force of nature. Just as I thought, replies the humanist, you are afraid. You think only of taking cover in religion. Renunciation is always an act of cowardice; it is we, the libertines, who dare to live dangerously. To live dangerously—that is the important thing. Yes, that is the only important thing. Not to be afraid of self, to have the strength and courage to contemplate your heart and body without disgust; to dare to impress your personality violently upon your contemporaries —and if you have genius, upon posterity itself—even though you may present the most shameful vices for their applause. From this point of view, St. Theresa or St. John of the Cross are no more impressive than Nero or Caesar Borgia, and were no more accomplished. And in the final analysis, it is the splendid

19

monsters who, having exposed themselves to the greater risks, deserve most to be admired.

That—to put it baldly—is the humanist point of view. In addressing a Spanish audience, obviously, I have no need to defend the saints against charges of weakness and cowardice. And indeed not only with regard to saints, but even the humblest Christian who strives to live by grace, there is obviously no question of fleeing for cover or protecting themselves from life's risks. No, it is a question of love. But when one speaks of love one speaks of suffering. And what love is more exacting than the unique love? The sanctification of a soul is a long, drawn out task, a day by day severance from the world that entails obscure struggles, a prolonged and silent heroism. It is quite the reverse of sleep, of nonexistence, of nothingness. Union with God is the fruit of a superhuman victory. Shelter and rest, indeed! At times, your valiant St. Theresa herself could not always suppress a cry of loving anguish: "O long life! O cruel life! O life in which I no longer live!"

Truly, is not she who uttered this cry as much possessed by an unearthly love as any humanist would dare to be by his earthly love when he attempts unaided to devise for himself a personal system of thought and conduct?

I believe so. I believe that no matter how firmly a man makes up his mind to be a technician, an engineer of living, he cannot escape the famous dilemma that St. Augustine posed: "Love of self carried to the point of contempt of God—love of God carried to the point of contempt for self." For we are not inert bodies that can be exposed harmlessly to the hazards of life. Human conscience is a fact; and it is a living world in itself with laws all its own which no one is at liberty to disregard on the excuse that his concern is solely with practical living. Some of the saints were kings, some soldiers, others were married; and while they performed their duties of state faultlessly, they never allowed these to alienate them from the inner world—that world of the spirit which offers signs to be interpreted, scents to be taken up, and trails to be followed, all of which perhaps will lead us where we would not choose to go.

As I see it, certain humanists make the mistake of believing themselves lord and master of this inner world, free to select some elements and to ignore others. For example they feel they can disregard laws whose existence a man so estranged from Christianity as Marcel Proust affirmed in a famous passage of *La Prisonnière*: "Everything in our life happens as if we had entered it burdened with obligations contracted in some previous existence. Given the conditions of human life, there is no reason in the world for us to feel that we are obliged to do good or be considerate of others. All these obligations which find no sanction in the present life seem to be part and parcel of a different world founded on goodness, sincerity, and sacrifice. It is a world altogether foreign to this one, a world that we left behind to be born on this earth, and will perhaps return to again, to live under the sway of those unknown laws which we have obeyed because we carried the knowledge of them in our hearts, without knowing who put it there. . . ." The Christian, however, knows what that world is; and how clear this revelation of conscience is in the light of the Revelation in history! How the voice of Christ in history harmonizes with that of the Christ within us! For the Christian, as well as the humanist, looks within himself for the makings of his personality. The whole difference is that he finds within him infinitely more than himself.

From St. Augustine to Pascal, from Newman to Maurice Blondel, the Church, as you know, has always had its apologists to point out to us where, in our innermost selves, the ascent to God begins. It is always through the medium of our personal life that we attain to the transcendent. "The supernatural is urgent within us." And faith springs from the union of this inner urgency and external Revelation. It springs from a conformity between the Christ of history, forever living and teaching in the Church, and the deepest aspirations of the human heart. The Christian is a humanist who does not stop at the surface manifestations of self, and who begins with the human side in order to surpass it. I accept humanity as a starting point, but humanity itself contains seeds of the divine. I deny there is any barrier between the ideal and the real. Reality is permeated with the ideal: "The Kingdom of God is within you."

To which, no doubt, the humanist will object that he detects no such inner exigency of God in himself; he finds no traces of the divine within. And he is right. But will the humanist deny that his whole intellectual and moral life begins with a deliberate negation of the supernatural? He affects a certain humility and reduces all to the business of practical living and the management of daily needs; his reasoning starts with a denial of God. This initial resistance to the transcendent, this impassioned denial preceding all other steps accounts for the insensitivity of so many modern thinkers to the things of God—a cultivated and acquired insensitivity. They have torn up beforehand every channel whereby grace might reach

23

71318

them. Nothing in the supernatural order can possibly affect them any longer, except for some thunderous intervention by God, like the thunderbolt that struck down St. Paul.

Whatever they say about it, even among the most hardened the longing for God betrays its presence under another guise. So as to get along without God more painlessly, they look for the equivalent of God in themselves. They reject the Infinite Being, but the obscure longing they feel for Him leads them to believe in their own ability to create the divine. "Ah yes," exclaims Ramón Fernández at the end of an admirable study of Newman, "the moment I reach the deepest level of my being, I feel myself impelled to hope, to will, and to believe in a world different from the one about me, and in a being different from myself. But does not this world already exist in my hope, my will, and my faith? Do not these aspirations which I find only within myself disclose another side of me, whether it be my self of tomorrow or a world where others like me will live one day? Do they not bring a message, these feelings which assail me from all sides, like the scent of a forest in the deep of night?" So he too catches these scents. Yet he denies that they originate anywhere but in himself, that beyond the shadowy forest a great light shines, and that beyond this deep night a great love awaits him.

The truth is that many people *repress* the longing for God. Repression, in the Freudian sense, has become a commonplace today. Every deviation from the normal is explained in terms of repressed sexual impulses. But few seem to have thought that perhaps the divine urgency within us can also be repressed. There is no other answer to the man who insists he has never felt this urgency within himself and who demands proof in terms of pure reason. But here I must make a confession.

As a novelist, I am used to living very close to the secret places of the heart and seeing everything in terms of the God of Pascal, "sensed by the heart, not by reason." So perhaps in this brief talk I have not sufficiently marked out the role of the intelligence in the search for God. Far from deprecating the value of intelligence, or speculative knowledge, Catholic philosophy in France today is the vanguard of the anti-Bergsonian and anti-pragmatist movements, thanks to the Thomist renascence, whose most distinguished protagonist among the laity is Jacques Maritain—not to mention certain eminent theologians, Dominican and Jesuit. No doubt, if philosophy were my profession, I would have accented that renascence. But, I repeat, I am only a novelist, decidedly ill at ease in the field of abstract logic and the concepts of Scholasticism.

Yes, a novelist. And here I must face an objection which anyone at all acquainted with my writings could hardly fail to formulate more or less precisely. Obviously, it is poor taste to talk of oneself, even though it is only to accuse oneself publicly. But how can I evade an objection that any opponent is bound to raise—unless he happens to be as courteous as Ramón Fernández?

Your whole effort as a novelist, my critics would say, gives a definite lie to what you have just told us. Your heroes and heroines are carnal creatures of insatiable cravings, and it would seem as if God Himself were powerless against the fire that consumes them, against the concupiscence that destroys them. Precisely with reference to the supernatural, they would say, your work demonstrates the inability of Catholicism to solve the problem of physical love. For to suppress a question is not to answer it. Catholicism does not give the flesh its due, but confuses it with evil; in fact, for a Catholic it is the evil of evils. Thus for many it has dried up, and for many others muddied, the one spring in which humanity has found a drop of joy. As a matter of fact, my opponent would add, not only is the flesh not evil, but nothing worthwhile can be accomplished without it on any level of activity. The great deeds and accomplishments which reflect most honor on the human race are the fruit of the ceaseless struggle to vindicate the claims of the flesh against a pitiless Christian asceticism.

I make no effort, you must admit, to tone down the objection. We must be honest about it, it is a strong one, and such as wins a hearing in every heart, even Christian. For what Christian at some moment or other has not endured the pangs of the flesh?

How could I deny it? It is quite true that as a novelist I have been highly sensitive to the atmosphere of my generation and of those post-war generations which had an André Gide, a Marcel Proust, and a Freud as mentors. In common with them, I have accorded altogether too much attention to physical love. Almost without realizing it, a novelist is a witness who enregisters the most secret stirrings of his times. And when our grandchildren come to form a judgment of our era, the thing that will astonish them most is the undue importance we have conceded to everything relating to physical love, our insistence on envisioning everything in reference to it and explaining all things in terms of it. Sex has become a fixation for a host of otherwise sensible people, who in any other age would surely not have made so much of it.

One of our moralists made the well known remark:

"Many a man would never have loved, if he had never heard speak of it!" No one can deny that there has been a great conspiracy, as it were, not only in the theatre, the cinema, in art, and in fiction, but in medicine and the healing arts as well, to keep this obsession alive among many who normally would scarcely have given it a thought—and especially to keep it alive beyond those short years of youth when the body is vigorous and pure, and when nature decrees that human couples should perpetuate the human race. Among uneducated people, among peasants who live close to the soil, it is a rare thing, once the time for love is past, for the passions to come back to trouble their middle age or later years.

A little while ago I spoke of the mania—given vogue by Freud's popularizers—of reducing everything in man to a repression of the sexual drive. But even if there are many repressed individuals among us, how many more who not only repress nothing but who give free rein to passions, which are, to say the least, unnatural, for having been deliberately aroused and provoked.

I realize this merely defines the problem without solving it. It would be useless to deny that on this point the Christian and the humanist are profoundly and basically at variance. If chastity, purity, and virginity are considered Christian values, if the union of man and woman—though raised to the dignity of a sacrament—is still zoned off by Church prohibitions and restrictions, that is because the entire mystery of the world's Redemption by the Son of God rests upon the mystery of the Original Fall. The Church does not trust the flesh because she knows that the flesh fell with Adam. The humanist, of course, holds this dogma in abhorrence; he denies that nature is vitiated. And our Montaigne asserts: "Absolute and godlike perfection consists in knowing how to enjoy one's self fully."

In an informal chat like the present one, we can merely establish the fact of this incurable opposition, without getting into a discussion that would lead us far afield. However, it can be said in support of the Christian point of view that the apparently excessive seriousness with which the Church views the carnal peril is justified by the facts. An English Catholic, Chesterton, said something to the effect that whenever something in Christianity seems extraordinary to us, in the end it is because there is something extraordinary in reality that corresponds to it. Undoubtedly, the importance Christianity gives to the flesh seems excessive. But there is, in fact, a force within the flesh that is equally inclined to excess. Previously I compared our instincts, our secret inclination to young and graceful animals with which man thinks he can safely play until the day when suddenly he finds himself face to face with a ferocious beast. I repeat, man is not a mere repair-mechanic faced with a machine that needs adjustment; he is an animal tamer facing wild beasts. It is a matter of daily observation that one can never do enough for the flesh, that it harbors a formidable energy, an appetite forever disappointed and never satisfied, an almost infinite insatiability.

To this the humanist is always free to reply, "Speak for yourself!" He can object that in every age there has always been a certain number of men who, while lacking in every vestige of religious belief, have known how to practise wisdom and moderate their desires. Stoic virtue is not an empty phrase, and the better part of humanity continues to endure hardship and abstain from all excesses without on that account professing any metaphysical reasons for doing so. There again I can only underline the opposition between Christian and humanist without pretending to settle it in a few words. The point I ought to develop, time permitting, is that the Christian above all realizes the weakness of human nature, the vastness of human misery; and that, on the other hand, the humanist always seems to be looking at the image of an abstract man, strong and well-balanced. The cross in every life, that personal, individual cross made to our measure, which each of us must sooner or later bear, the humanist does not see. He refuses to see it.

Once more, I do not mean to belittle an opponent who is often of heroic stature. Apart from any religious faith, we are all acquainted with souls that are naturally righteous, noble through and through— souls that bring to our lips Polyeuctus' prayer for Pauline:*

> *Lord, in thy goodness grant me this,*
> *She is too virtuous not to be a Christian.*
> *Thou hast fashioned her with too much care*
> *Not to let her know thee and love thee.*

Yes, wisdom is no idle word, and it is that imprint of God in the non-Christian world that I love best. But much as I admire wisdom, it is a long way from sanctity. There is the whole distance of love.

Like most of my contemporaries, I neglected in my works to draw the necessary distinctions between instinct and love. But Christianity, while putting us fearfully on our guard against that instinct we have in common with the animals, on the other hand en-

* *Polyeucte* (Corneille.)

31

trusts the Infinite to our faculty of love. One need know only a few lives of those myriad saints, who are Christ's witnesses and recruits in the world, to smile at the charge of constraint and impoverishment with which the humanist reproaches Catholicism. The news Christ came to bring men is that they are not alone, that they are loved, that each of them in particular is loved. There is no greater love than to give one's life for one's friends. Everyone of the faithful knows he is the recipient of this immense predilection; and many have responded with the total gift. I am amazed that so many people are scandalized by the human element in the Church—abuses, sins, betrayals—in my view, the history of the Church becomes more and more the history of her saints; the mystery of the Church merges with the mystery of Jesus. For me it is enough to know that it is in the Church and through the Church, thanks to the sacraments she dispenses, that such perfect union with God could be achieved as that of Francis of Assisi, Catherine of Sienna, Theresa of Avila, the Curé of Ars. Those dogmas against which there is no appeal, that strict moral code—from that soil alone, and no other, such immeasurable loves have flowered, such spiritual nuptials wherein the creature becomes lost in the Creator are consummated.

And so it is that alleged weaklings and cowards who, the humanist insists, take refuge in religion to be at ease, are called, are led into a life of excess; for in God alone every excess is permissible. They embark upon a vast adventure, but not at the price of self-mutilation; they go into it whole and entire, with all their powers intact and with all their passions transfigured.

The miracle of it is that, though the summit of the spiritual life is attainable only to a smaller number, there is no one who is not called to undertake it. The miracle is that the most average Christian—as long as he retains his good will and does not neglect the sacraments, the source of grace—can pick up bits and morsels, and even more, from the same banquet table at which God satiates His saints. The simplest believer can have a foretaste of what the heroic St. Theresa experienced. Not only can he have it, he should have it. We are not free to love or not to love; to each of us individually St. John of the Cross addressed his warning: "At the end of this life you will be judged according to your love." You understand what love St. John is speaking of here. Many who think themselves furthest from experiencing it are perhaps closer to it than they dare imagine.

In all human love there is a deep-seated conflict,

a disproportion between the demands of the human heart and the creature to which it attaches itself; all novelists have devoted themselves to bringing this fact to light. Paul Claudel says with penetrating insight that woman is not happiness but a substitute for happiness. Sometimes, like Don Juan de Manara, man flits from creature to creature in quest of that mysterious and inaccessible joy; sometimes he settles down in marriage to look for happiness with one, and this is the commoner lot. If we are to believe the fiction writers who make marriage their theme, happy marriages are rare indeed, and the wonder of it is that so many couples survive the day to day misunderstandings. If each spouse stands by the other, in spite of everything, it is because creatures have an innate instinct for cleaving to one being and becoming one with it. We can see, even in the case of the more carnal, this latent urgency of contemplating one alone, of uniting with one only, which marriage almost always fails to fulfill. We cling desperately to that phantom of an only love because we were created for the Unique Love.

You are tempted, I am sure, to ask me what hope I still hold for a return of French intellectuals to the Church. You will remind me that even if influential personalities are returning, if men like Paul Claudel,

Jacques Maritain, Maurice Blondel, and many others, have become the nucleus of an ardent movement, they figure small indeed against the setting of the whole of contemporary philosophy, which is so brazenly indifferent, so hostile, as in my own country, to spirituality in any form.

I admit that is true. Of all the obstacles that Christianity encounters in the case of many intellectuals the most serious is doubtless the one I have already pointed out: they have lost the sense of human weakness. They fail to grasp the deeper meaning of St. Beuve's remark: "Life is a contest that must always be lost." Stoic virtue is a desperate lie that must be maintained at all cost, not only in face of illness and old age, defections and betrayals, in face of death itself, but above all in face of those appetites man gratifies in secret, in face of that vast taint which from adolescence to senility creeps over our entire being. So the time almost always arrives when in order to save face they are forced to deny that this stain is a stain at all, and to assert that evil is evil.

The Christian, in contrast, recognizes the fact of human frailty. To Nietzsche, who sets up a race of slaves as opposed to a race of masters or rulers, the Christian replies that there are no masters, that all are slaves of the flesh—but that it rests in our power to achieve freedom in Christ. Why speak of human sorrow? Life for us is no longer a contest always lost, but one arranged for us to win.

Time works for the Christian. As years pass and the storms of youth subside, and nature itself calms the impulses of flesh and blood, the Christian in the state of grace puts a gradually stronger accent on spiritual values. And the Spirit falls heir to all that lust forsakes.

Far more than his opponent the Christian is a man of progress, literally and in the truest sense of the term. Others believe solely in material progress, progress in external space; we believe in inner progress which is the sole reality.

Our idea of progress is fully expressed in Jacqueline Pascal's observation that "no limits can be placed on purity or on perfection." Even a St. John of the Cross or an Ignatius Loyola never completed the task of becoming saints. We need never fear that the saints will distract mankind from its temporal duties. There will always be plenty of technicians to take care of the affairs of this world, but there will never be enough sanctity here below to counterbalance that raging concupiscence which leads to such fearful destruction. I must say I cannot understand how anyone today could fear an excess of spirituality in the world.

This essential human wretchedness from which the saints forge their victories and triumphs, remains forever incomprehensible to many intellectuals. They are inclined to place their faith in a purely human virtue; but in order not to see its fragility, they must close their eyes to their own failures, their own decadence. And when this ruse is no longer possible, and their decadence has become a spectacle for all men to see, they glory in it and convince themselves that it is not decadence at all, but goodness itself. "The light has come into the world," said Christ to Nicodemus, "yet men loved the darkness rather than the light, for their works were evil. For everyone who does evil hates the light." Yes, men love the darkness better than the light, and this is the eternal passion of Christ in the world until the end of time.

For a great many of our thinkers it is axiomatic that philosophy is a search—not a discovery. It is a game in which one may seek but must never find, except by cheating. To the savants of our century, and in fact almost every century, what is inexplicable and merits death is the simple affirmation of Christ's: "I am the Truth." Pilate's question: "What is truth?" has been picked up again by the modern world, and with the very inflection of the procurator of Judea so as to infer once again that it admits no reply.

Long ago when Christ declared that He was the Bread of Life, the Living Bread come down from heaven that gives itself for the life of the world, many disciples finding this a hard saying walked no more with Him. Only a small group of apostles remained, and the words Christ spoke to them on that occasion are those which I find more moving perhaps than any in the entire Gospel: "Do you also wish to go away?" Do you also wish to go away? Thus will the Creator entreat his creatures until the end of time.

Among our intellectuals, is it the little flock or is it the vast throng which replies with St. Peter: "To whom shall we go? Thou hast words of everlasting life." Unquestionably, the little flock. But what does the future hold in store? When the Church is in question, words like victory and defeat no longer retain their customary meaning. Never do we find her so helpless as in her triumphs, nor so powerful as in her humiliations. Until the consummation of the world we shall always find the same tumult around the Cross, the same welter of insults and mockery, and in particular, the same indifference of Pilate, the same thrust of the lance by the careless hand. But there will also be the prayer of the penitent thief, the tears of Magdalen, the centurion's act of faith, the silent devotion of the beloved disciple. Each of us must choose which role he will play in this eternal drama; no one can avoid playing a part. To refuse to choose is in itself a choice. You may believe yourself free to assume a distinterested attitude toward the Absolute. But what assurance have you that the Absolute takes no interest in you? That is the important thing.

The demands of modern life in no wise require us to repudiate the eternal claims of God within us. It is not within our province to renounce the Absolute, or simply decide to devote ourselves to something else. For Christ or against Christ—we are bound to choose. Failure to take sides is to have made a choice: "He who is not with me is against me . . ." Happy are those to whom it is given to understand that apart from Him there is nothing.

II

What Can Christians Hope for on Earth? *

HAVE Christians a hope for this world? Actually, since the Christian is a man who believes he is also a man who hopes, and not alone for happiness in another life. The essence of our hope is its indivisibility: it is concerned with time because it is concerned with eternity. There is no contradiction between our belief in a Father Who is in heaven and the coming of His kingdom on earth. We claim rather that the contradiction is all on the side of the atheist, for we can see no reasonable grounds for a temporal hope on the part of anyone who lacks faith in eternal life.

Today the fraud has been unmasked which not so long ago opposed the Nietzschean cult of youth and strength to the religion of the vanquished and the

* Text of a lecture given at the Conference of Catholic Intellectuals of 1951.

misfits branded with the sign of the Cross. Who will deny that the despair of this generation is fostered by Zarathustra's, "God is dead," that mournful cry which has been taken up and orchestrated anew by the young masters this generation has taken to heart?

If there is no God and everything, therefore, is permitted, the first thing permitted is despair. The first morose pleasure of the melancholy heart is to indulge in the intoxicating notion that the world is absurd, and that there is no point in our being less absurd than the world. Hope, like faith—hope, here and now—is a theological virtue. The Christian is obliged to hope just as he is to be chaste, or to refrain from hatred. Despair is a luxury we cannot indulge in, a temptation to which we are commanded not to yield. And how strange that it assails us in youth more than at any other times. How strange that at twenty we shed our bitterest tears; and now that life begins to fade a degree of calmness comes, an acceptance of all that has been, that is, and that will be, an intuitive grasp of what Bernanos meant when he put those sublime words in the mouth of his dying country curé, "All is grace!" Yes, all is grace here on earth. We know this, and we believe it, and at odd moments we experience it in prayer or in the heart to heart intimacy of a Communion.

41

If God does not exist, and the world is without direction or goal, if it comes from nothing and leads nowhere, and if man is trapped in the dreary mechanisms of his daily work, a mere cog in a machine—whether serving private interests in a capitalist system or serving the party or the State in a collectivist regime—then the man of today remains alien to those things that make up the grim and monotonous course of his daily life. His mind which reasons and reflects, his heart which longs and suffers, that part of him, in sum, that is essentially himself, is not in the least concerned with the nuts and bolts he tightens, the tickets he punches, or the columns of figures he adds in ledgers. If Christ is not risen and if our hope is vain, every man is literally a prisoner. Even the privileged few who escape from the shackles of forced labor fall prey perhaps to a worse bondage, for there are prisoners of pleasure and automatons of vice.

I am well aware that for a large portion of humanity today a great hope has crystallized around Communism. Yes, of course. Yet, by the very fact that Stalinist Communism is identified with materialism, its earthly hope is inwardly nourished, if I may say, by a despair that limits it and hems it in on every side. What despair? That which necessarily flows from the proposition that spirit does not exist independently of the body, but is merely a secondary

42

factor, a function of the brain, and that the material world perceived by our senses is the sole reality. Certainly, we can see how Communism provides the inmates of this materialist prison with a motive for awaiting oblivion. Of all the ways of "softening the bed of straw," to use Vigny's phrase, probably the most tempting is, in effect, to work toward a future in which the overfed will be made to disgorge, and in which production and consumption will be regulated according to the laws of justice. To say nothing of the fact that while awaiting the return to nothingness it may be quite satisfying to feel oneself in tune with History, and belong to the Party—a worldly power aimed at nothing less than the domination of the world. Yes, it may be highly satisfying, even thrilling, to be part of an enterprise with the whole planet for its stage and the human race as its prize! And still, in the end, what does it all mean to the individual, destined to disappear altogether? The party, the party's struggles, its triumphs, will have helped him to keep going, true. But his joy will have been of a stereotyped kind, much like that of the boys and girls we see grinning from ear to ear amid the fields of wheat in all publications of totalitarian propaganda. It is not the inner joy, the only one that counts, true joy, our joy.

This joy of ours is noticed by our generation more

than we Christians think. From time to time I am asked if I feel there is a religious revival underway. Well, no, not exactly a revival; let us say rather an interest, a nostalgia. I know more than one atheist who loiters on the outskirts of the humbled and huddled flock we form. A flock, alas—we can say these things among ourselves—that is not always the sort to attract outsiders overmuch. For we also are practised in the law that withers and the letter that kills, yes, that has not ceased to kill even yet. . . . But despite all this, something else remains, thank God, which it is not in our power to destroy, something which in spite of our mediocrity we carry within us, and which without our realizing it shines forth. It is that fire which Our Lord came on earth to kindle, and which at this moment of time it is our turn to keep aglow as best we know how, that fire which keeps the animals away but attracts souls that feel cold.

Souls that feel cold . . . There are many today. There was a time, perhaps in a Huysman's day, when the Catholic liturgy was a beacon light guiding writers and artists to the Church; and I personally can testify to what the prestige of men like Peguy, of Claudel, and later of Maritain, did to keep us faithful in the dark days of Combism and of our own twenty years. Today, however, young people rarely read Huysman; Peguy and Bernanos are dead; Maritain is across the sea; and the patriarchal Claudel is gathering in his final sheaves.* No witness of great stature has arisen this mid-century to voice his belief that the Son of Man is the Son of God. It must mean, therefore, that the Son of Man has no need of any witnesses but us, or rather, but Himself in us—so striking is the contrast between us who put our faith in the *Pater* we recite and who believe in the Father Who is Love and in His risen Son, between us who have remained faithful, and this generation which keeps alive all the myths our fathers found so stimulating, this rather frantic generation which has pitched its tent under the sign of the absurd at the meeting place where all the pernicious ideologies of the past century have finally converged. Marxism has been tried out wherever Soviet Russia rules, and millions toil there at forced labor to make men happier on earth. At Hiroshima and in the laboratories of germ warfare, science fulfills the promise made at its beginnings: "You will be like gods . . ." The religion of Progress and of human perfectibility is pondered at leisure by survivors of concentration camps and by "displaced persons" lodged in their parti-

* Mr. Claudel died on February 23, 1955 (Transl. note).

tioned barracks, who have left the cadavers of their children behind them under the rubble of their ruined cities—not to mention those martyrs of warring ideologies who have filled, and still fill, the prisons of Europe to overflowing.

We Christians who held fast to our hope, to our enchantment amidst a disenchanted world can begin to understand why we embody humanity's last chance when we contemplate the state of despair that has overtaken mankind in our day and age. A day and age when one can no longer find a single Socialist with the faith of a Jaurés or a single Communist who feels a personal bond with the cause of Slav imperialism which he serves; when the world of the concentration camp outlives the infamous regime that gave it birth, and when in Russia the exploitation of man is without redress (since it is no longer the employing class that exploits him, but the proletarian party itself, impeccable, infallible, and unlimited in prerogative).

Hope here on earth? Yes, here on earth. I have not forgotten the question I was asked to answer: Have Christians a temporal hope? What my questioners probably meant was: Have Christians a political hope? Here I shall answer as a man for whom hope (except perhaps at the time of Liberation, and then only for a few weeks) was never political. Understand me. I believe that Christian hope is concerned with time, and with politics too, but as an antidote to a poison. If there is one lesson that history has never tired of teaching us, it is that the condition of Christianity is worse when Christians hold political power. Political Christianity, that is to say, the spiritual power of the Church placed at Caesar's service and the formidable arm of Caesar placed at the service of the Church, has always had deplorable results, especially in the France and Spain of the sixteenth and seventeenth centuries, and even since then . . . But these are burning questions affecting wounds not fully healed. Let me merely point out that when we say that Christian hope does not lie in the political order, this does not mean that we should renounce politics, for to attempt to avoid political action is the worst kind of politics. In most cases one can avoid it only by an attitude of self-complacency, by keeping silent, and by acting as an accomplice without assuming any risk.

At a time when in so large a part of the planet all thought—including the research of the scientists and the inspiration of the poet—is supervised, slanted and controlled, it is we who believe in the word of Christ, whatever our political allegiance, who share

the earthly hope of preserving in the world the in-
violable conscience of man. This earthly hope of
Christians in the political sphere is, in fact, much
more than just a hope. It is a certainty we have here
on earth that as long as there remains in the world a
Christian worthy of the name—yes, even if there
were only one—there will remain an inner life to
which no police can ever force entry.

Ah, you Catholics who are listening to me, how I
should like to make you aware this evening of the
immense happiness, the immense opportunity that
has been given to our generation. We Catholics of
1951 are sons of a Church which to our forefathers
of the Eighteenth and Nineteenth centuries repre-
sented the enslavement of the mind, but which today
is freedom incarnate, even in the eyes of non-
believers. The slandered Church of the *Syllabus* now
shows its true face to the world. "The truth will set
you free"—today we know that this is literally a fact.
The Nazis found it out, just as the Stalinists are
finding it out again. Wherever a Christian conscience
exists, a secret dialogue, a silent interchange will go
on—a tryst that no Caesar can surprise, before which
he remains powerless. These intimacies between
Creator and creature have in days past found the
prisons their favorite spot, and they still do today.

48

Only yesterday, as I read a letter from a prisoner I do not know, I could not take my eyes off the three letters PAX surmounted by a little cross at the top of the cheap lined page. I did not worry about the fate of that prisoner. He had achieved that state of which Pascal tells us, where one has passed beyond the possibility of hurt or help at the hands of men—more than that, where all the harm they can do us is transformed into love.

And that is why all the techniques of the totalitarians will always be bent upon forcing the door of this last sanctuary of mankind: the Christian conscience. And indeed, they appear to succeed when their prisoner, struck at the very point where the soul and mind meet, stands before his judges witless and broken. Yes, but even then, in spite of his torturers, and perhaps without realizing it himself, a Cardinal Mindszenty turns defeat into victory, because he raises before the world the living image of his Crucified Lord.

That we have the right to hope politically I believe with all my heart. And still, it is a mystery to me—seeing the age I have reached and all these eyes have seen—how devout Christians can look for anything better than the return of the Lord, or how they can bother their heads about anything except putting all in readiness for it, though it be thousands of years away. So as to answer in advance the painful question that Jesus once asked: "When the Son of Man comes will he find faith on the earth?" Is this any different from saying: "Will he find hope on earth?" For despair grows, as you can see, to the extent that atheism is victorious, and the world it fashions is a world grown absurd in the eyes of men without God.

Naturally, we cannot help having political preferences. I have nursed some all my life. I could well say of myself what Lacordaire said: that he would die a penitent Christian and an impenitent liberal. Political preferences, then, but not a political hope—and preferences, moreover, that we should control, closely guard, and hold in check. Ah, if only the young people listening would think over carefully what I have said, whether they incline to the positivism of the extreme right wing or yield to the lure of Marxism. To belong to a party of either extreme means accepting orders and obeying commands. With any such party, you run the risk of espousing lies and hate—most of all hate. You can be sure that an apostle, whether layman or priest, who lives his faith to the full, serves the political cause he favors better than any partisan zealot. Who, for instance, has worked harder for the proletariat than the elite of our younger clergy? and I am not only referring to the priests who have gone into the factories as workers.* Who has done more for the working class than numerous laymen, both men and women, particularly those of the J.O.C. movement?** Truly, the politics of this model Church we have in France is wholly taken up with the quest of souls, with opening up channels through which grace may flow everywhere, even to places most difficult of access, in order to reach souls there and save what was lost.

There is a basic contradiction between the political life directed wholly at the outer world and the Christian life directed wholly at what lies within. No matter how much a Christian, whether priest or layman, lives for his brothers and with his brothers, sharing their troubles and subjecting himself to the same tasks, still it is only within himself that he seeks and finds the kingdom of God. I imagine (and I ask your pardon for daring to speak of such matters)

* The author's several references to the priest-worker movement in this book were made prior to the difficulties in which some members of this apostolate became involved, and to the Church's curtailment of it. (Transl. note)

** The J.O.C. (Jeunesse Ouvrière Chrétienne) signifies the Young Christian Workers movement, which concerns itself with applying Catholic social principles to the workers and their problems. (Transl. note) that it must be communion with God through meditation, prayer, and the sacraments, that it must be the life of grace within him that nourishes his apostolic efforts and makes them bear fruit. I imagine that this hidden and deeply buried source of spiritual living, known and accessible only to himself and to God, is what he must preserve most jealously.

For me, the temporal expectation of a Christian, his hope here on earth—and I know no other—is never to lose or, if he has had the misfortune of losing it, to regain the foretaste of his eternal hope: that inner calm, that peace which the world cannot give, but which the world can so promptly take away. In the midst of the worst disasters of history and despite all the sins of one poor life, this inner silence contains the voice that reassures us, and through us reassures the whole world . . . Do you recall it? The words of Our Lord as He walked upon the turbulent sea, and called out to the poor creatures trembling in their boat? "It is I, do not be afraid."

III

*Is Christian Civilization in Peril?**

Is WESTERN civilization threatened? It may seem
strange that we even trouble to ask the question,
what with the Red Army camped at our doors and
able, if it set out tonight, to parade down the streets
of Brussels and Paris tomorrow morning. Moreover,
can we still speak of a threat at all? Has not the threat
been carried out already? Belgium twice invaded, occupied, and oppressed, France with the wounds in
her side still open, Germany in ruins, are there to
testify that on the day the Asiatic armies of Russia
sweep across Europe, they would only pile ruin on
top of ruin, only reopen ancient and half-healed
wounds. They would not destroy Western civilization, but merely complete its destruction. They

* Text of a discourse given at Brussels in 1948 on the occasion of
the *Grandes Conferences Catholiques.*

would knock down the remnants of a sublime structure already riddled with termites from within.

If by Western civilization we mean that which was born of the fusion of the Gospel of the Son of God with the wisdom of the great men of ancient Athens and Rome, that heritage of ideas, beliefs, morals and customs which our forefathers have handed down for a thousand years, we must admit that the physical ravages which afflict Europe today are only the outward signs of a destruction more hidden and more to be feared. Although for the time being we can sleep elsewhere than in cellars, although we are enjoying a respite, and although the planes that bombed our cities have been consigned to the scrap pile, their task accomplished, and the models that are to replace them are not as yet quite perfected, although, in short, the visible destruction of Europe has been halted for a time, the spiritual ravages continue nevertheless to reach new depths. Certainly it is an understatement to say they are most serious; for the very destiny of the civilization we are discussing this evening hinges on whether they wax or wane.

It would matter little if all our Churches were levelled to the ground providing the truths that built them still lived in the heart of Western man. If the faith of our fathers, which has moved more than mountains and caused our Cathedrals to spring from the heart of Europe—some few of which happily have escaped the blows of both our enemies and our friends—if that faith, I say, were still alive in us, it would bring forth new miracles of stone, and perhaps even of concrete. Many Cathedrals at which we marvel are built on the site of still older basilicas which must also have been very beautiful themselves; yet our fathers thought nothing of razing them, or did not take the trouble to restore them, because they knew that they bore in their hearts the threefold source of all creativity: faith, hope, and love. Is there enough of that love, hope, and faith still left in our hearts, to enable us to rebuild what has been destroyed, in the spiritual as well as the material order, even though atheism, hatred, and despair are once more preparing to destroy them? Our fate depends on the answer we can give to this question.

In France we have all laughed a great deal at the American soldier's remark about our ruined Churches: "We'll build much nicer ones for you. . . ." Yet that naive remark is not so funny as it seems. It expresses a profound truth. Namely, that a nation which has confidence in its own civilization has no reason for clinging to the relics of the past.

The antiquarian spirit of Europeans today is an alarming sign of age and impotence. It testifies to the fear that their source of strength has dried up. The young American, bursting with confidence in himself and looking wholly toward the future, can be flippant about our ancient and gloomy Churches, every stone, every slab of which is hallowed for us. We should not be hard on him for his disdain that is a sign of his youthful vigor.

Unfortunately, for ills of the spirit America has only material remedies to offer us. Not that we can scorn them! Understand me: I have no taste for the role of the ungrateful beggar; and while it may be true that man does not live by bread alone, he lives by bread first of all. Starving Europe ought to speak only with gratitude and friendship about those who feed her.

But, in the end, Occidental civilization does not find its full expression in machine-tools, nor in refrigerators, nor in any of those manufactured goods, which force their makers to find markets for them or perish. The forces in a moribund Europe that still resist death do not originate in America, but here, in Belgium, in Holland, in Switzerland, in Italy, in Spain, in Portugal, in Germany, in the Scandinavian countries, in Great Britain, in France; in this Europe,

of which America is now more than ever the tribu-
tary. For she, also, would die the same death, if the
fire that Europe lit and kept alight for a thousand
years should fail; America, too, would perish of the
cold. America is but an offshoot of ours, a formidable
one, to be sure; but its sap still flows into it from the
age-old trunk; and she in turn is already—and un-
wittingly—suffering from our exhaustion.

This fact helps us to understand why to many
countries France, though humiliated, in ruins, pos-
sessing the mere shadow of an army and a navy, and
floundering in disorders and internal confusion, still
stands—and perhaps more than ever before—as the
nation from which we can look with hope for those
things which wealthier and more industrialized nations cannot give. And when I say France, it is
European Christianity I have in mind, of which you
Belgian Catholics comprise one of the most illustrious branches; it is European humanism which your
artists have so magnificently enriched.

Here is the point I feel should by all means be
emphasized: it is we the Europeans, despite our collapse, upon whom the responsibility for Western
civilization still rests. The aid we receive from across
the Atlantic will help us enormously; in fact, it is
indispensable. Nevertheless, it would be of little help

if we failed at the same time to take cognizance of the fact that in the spiritual struggle which divides the world the spiritual weapons to be used have been entrusted to us from the start, and first of all to us, the Catholics of Gaul.

In a sense, we might say that we Catholics are the beneficiaries of the dramatic events through which the human race is living, since what is happening confirms what we have believed. The present era is like a great crossroads upon which all roads have ominously converged ever since, through Nietzsche's voice, men proclaimed the death of God. In this universe of horrors where the will to power of two opposing empires lines up the human robots on two sides, it seems, as Saint Theresa said, that we have gone infinitely far from what we have desired. Our forefathers dreamed of relieving man of the weight of his oppressing circumstances, and man has become the mere human material from which the anonymous divinities of the State exact nothing but efficient production—and then, when the day of reckoning with the rival race arrives, the acceptance without murmur of his final immolation.

Science, which our fathers deified and in which they invested all their hopes for a paradise, and perhaps immortality, here on earth is becoming each day our most effective death-dealing instrument. And this is stating it mildly, when we consider that the very planet itself is in danger of dissolution and annihilation.

Everything is happening as though the Infinite Being, to convince us, Cartesians that we are, is resorting to the criterion of evidence—evidence that a world without God is a world condemned to turn its own genius against itself. So much so, in fact, that the slightest advance in the discovery or the mastery of nature's laws cannot be made without its becoming another step toward the destruction of the species.

Yes, God's witnesses have the consolation today of not only believing, but seeing and touching, if I dare say it, the fact that when He in Whom they believe said: "I am the life," it should have been taken literally, and in the most physical sense of the word. "The misery of man without God": how feeble that phrase of Pascal's sounds today! Misery is the very least we can say. With love vanishing from the earth, man has become just one more species among all others in the vegetal and animal world which mutually devour one another.

As Christians, we confirm the fact that History has proven us to be right. We confirm it, however, without pride or self satisfaction but with a sense of shame and anguish. For all the horrors that have come upon the world have occurred only because of our spiritual poverty; and this is not the least of our crimes. Before Western civilization was threatened by the Red army, by Marxism, or by atheistic Existentialism, it was first threatened inwardly in the Christian conscience. Those whose mission it was to keep the fire aglow let it die out. All those victories of death over life during the last century and a half were won thanks to our incurable phariseeism, and thanks especially to the failures of political Catholicism—failures which Karl Marx turned so prodigiously to his own advantage.

In these few moments, I can only suggest to you a few themes for meditation, a few threads of thought. I should like you to think about this last point at your leisure, for I cannot develop this highly controversial question without giving offense and reopening certain wounds.

No, it is not with satisfaction or complacency that Catholics consider themselves trustees of the salvation of the human race, even in the temporal sphere. For they cannot at the same time fail to recognize their own tragic failure to adapt to the needs of modern society. Too often they feel cut off from their times, as though isolated in a sort of Christian ghetto. Sometimes they have the feeling that grace is distributed to mankind only through old, out-of-date conduits half clogged up with the rust of centuries.

At this point, however, let us hasten to add that some changes are in progress. One of the most hopeful signs is the splendid effort of the Catholic hierarchy to revitalize the methods of the apostolate, an effort which not so long ago would have been viewed as imprudent, even rash. Yes, judging by what is happening in France today, a great hope has been raised. The sordid garage of Montreuil, where a priest of the *Mission de Paris* celebrates Mass and explains it to a crowd to which no one had ever before spoken of Christ, this garage, I say, shines in the eyes of God with a brilliance perhaps greater than that of Notre Dame de Chartres. In the economy of grace perhaps those little bands of Dominican friars which evangelize our dechristianized countryside occupy a higher place than our most famous Abbeys. Who can say that their poor hymns do not swell in eternity with a quality unequalled by the albums of Solesmes?

Yet on one crucial point we have to admit a serious falling off. From the beginning of the last century up to our own generation, Catholicism has been able, despite a materialism triumphant on every side, to count among her apologists minds of the highest inspiration. From Chateaubriand and De-Maistre, from Lamennais and Lacordaire, to Huysmans, to Bloy, to Claudel, to Peguy—the intellectual leaders in whom the youth of my country confided were disciples of Christ. And yesterday again, in the assemblies of UNESCO, held in Mexico, by all accounts it was the voice of our Jacques Maritain that was listened to more than any other, and that struck the deepest chords in the hearts and minds of the participants.

It may be that I am incapable of recognizing the teams on our side. But after all, faced as we are today my Marxists, atheistic Existentialists, pseudo-Surrealists, whom have the younger generation produced that can speak with the power and authority of a Peguy or a Claudel? It may well be that from now on we need only saints. And already we can see this modern sanctity taking shape little by little; we begin to see its true features in the city streets, the suburbs, and in our countrysides. Now that France in many of her Provinces has become a missionary land once more, the apostles of the new times are taking on the features of those who at Christianity's dawn evangelized a world in which the Name that is above all names was heard for the first time.

I should like to be able to end on this note of hope, but what is the use of closing our eyes? The saints sow their seeds, but the sowers of weeds mingle with them, and the master they serve is at our gates with his countless army. In my homeland, Marxism has apparently reached its peak, and I doubt that it will make further gains. Its strength today rests on the Red army, and the strength of the Red army in turn rests on Russia, that immense, oppressed and unhappy land, of which as much as a century ago the Marquis de Custine wrote: "By a degrading submissiveness at home she is paying in advance for her hope of imposing tyranny on other countries." What the Marquis wrote of the Russia of the Czars applies exactly as well to the Russia of the Soviets. It is as true today as a hundred years ago that "to compensate the loss of all his freedom, public and personal, the kneeling slave dreams of conquering the world."

Obviously, there is an equal and probably superior power pitted against Asia. But, how else would Asia move but by first occupying all of Europe? And what good would it be to us if America, after years of preparation, landed her troops here merely to liberate cemeteries and ruins?

Still we should not believe that war is inevitable. No war is inevitable, as long as human free will remains one of the essential ingredients of History.

And there is something else in which we believe, and that is divine grace. Let us carry on, then, as if Western civilization were not going to perish, let us strive to lead it back to the source of living waters from which it has drawn its power and its glory. But let us act also as if our civilization might be attacked at any moment from without just as it is every moment from within. Each one of us should always have in mind this question: How can we preserve the peace? Since war today, whatever its outcome, would annihilate us.

Two theories confront us. Either Soviet Russia has already secretly decided upon war, as Hitler did long before Munich, and is simply waiting for the propitious moment—particularly the American crisis that she has been counting on, and that would leave her free to act. With Europe occupied, the Soviet government may think its exhausted and terrorized nations would prefer anything to the Apocalypse of an Anglo-Saxon landing; and that would be the moment for Russia to reach an understanding with the United States of America for dividing the world into two parts.

On the other hand, Soviet Russia dreads a war, but at the same time fears having it thrust upon her by a rival. She is haunted by that fear of encirclement which drove imperialist Germany to the aggression

64

of 1914. According to this second theory, each of the two Empires would live in terror of the other, and the danger of war would be born one day from this mutual terror.

Peace will be preserved, and our civilization with it, as long as Russia considers the Western world to be impregnable, and as long as she fears exhausting herself hopelessly, not so much against what is left of Christian and humanist Europe, as against its formidable American offspring. It is the task of Western diplomacy to convey to Soviet Russia the impression that we have not locked and bolted the door. We must let her know that, contrariwise, if the bolt is fastened on her side, it is not on ours, and that we are always ready to welcome Holy Russia again into the European family.

Unfortunately, nations do not change very easily. And how could they change when their geographical and ethnological conditions remain the same? Like the Russia of the Romanovs, the Russia of Stalin rules its people with so heavy a hand that the very survival of the regime requires that all its subjects be denied all contact with free nations. And this is even more the case today than under the Czars, when at least the nobility could know Europe and be exposed to its influence. Today the Russian people live, work, and suffer as if on another planet.

So let us not hope too much to avert by diplomatic means the menace that hangs over us. But as long as war has not engulfed us, we can take advantage of them. The nations of the West must stand constantly at attention, alert to the flood-gates in the very heart of Europe, extending from Prague to Budapest, which could burst open in an instant and send across our civilization a dreadful flood today—yes, infinitely more dreadful than in the days of Genghis Khan. For there is no nightmare more terrifying to the Humanist and the Christian than the spectre of this Asiatic tidal wave equipped by modern science.

The unity of Europe should be born of this threat. Already the Western statesmen have no choice but to adopt a common foreign policy. The imminence of the danger is great enough to bring about a renascence of Christianity. In the past it was the Arabs, then the Turks, whose mere presence at our gates brought into existence our ever vigilant Europe. Their presence alone created that Western chivalry always ready to give its life, that world so quickened, alert, and taut, where every person counts because he has an immortal soul, where the mind is free, and where genius flowers without having to account to anyone or follow any party line, where honor is the only rule imposed on everyone.

66

Oh, I am well aware that Western Christendom has not been a world without crime. Graham Greene was right to remind us that Christendom has committed practically the same crimes that we have seen flourish in Germany—and, alas, not in Germany alone. The point is, however, that Christendom was a world where evil remained evil and where, as Graham Greene phrases it in a striking epigram: "The possibility of great repentance was equalled by the possibility of great crime,"—whereas we live in a world where evil has been made the good. There is nothing sadder in the world than to see what we have seen and still see—the crime of the totalitarians who mobilize in their service the generosity of youth, and its spirit of sacrifice, and that greatest love of all, which is the gift of life itself. . . .

We have to rebuild Christendom. And, undoubtedly, we cannot hope to do this by artificially piecing together our broken society. The Christendom must be reshaped from its foundations. It is not a matter of building dams against Communism; dams always end up by being swept away. We have to pit one hope against the other, a new world order against the terrible order which rules in Moscow, and which through the intermediary of the national Communist parties, rules also in Belgrade, in Sophia, in Budapest, and in Bucharest, as it would rule tomorrow in Brussels, Paris, and Rome, should the delegates of the Kominform seize power there.

In Russia class struggle has produced only the semblance of a classless society. Actually, it is the same people—the most inured to suffering in the world—whom the eternal Czar, the eternal Peter the Great sacrifices to the Slavic will to power. There is, of course, something impressive in the scale of the undertaking being worked out in Eastern Europe. Our own should be equally gigantic in scale. It would be naive to imagine, as some men do who fancy themselves shrewd and realistic, that one can change the course of history with dollars and that gold is the final answer to everything. The war that ranges continents against each other today is a religious war. Of course, sordid interests also enter in, as they have in every crusade. But that does not prevent it from being a clash of ideas. We must not forget that the enemy's ideas are everywhere and always working on the minds and hearts of men, and in America too. Russia will never forsake the hope of seeing her enemy crumble from within. She has in her service termites slowly and patiently gnawing at the main girders. Patiently, ah yes! Patience is a virtue which the Russians have practiced for as long as they have known oppression, that is to say, as long as they have lived.

It is important that we also be moved by a spiritual principle capable of acting upon minds and hearts we are unable to reach directly. We have no iron curtain against Communism. But, on the other hand, there is no iron curtain, thank God, that a passion for liberty and a respect for the human being created in the image and likeness of God cannot pierce; there is no iron curtain against an ineradicable Christian hope.

It is not the kingdoms of this world, I realize, to whom it was promised that the gates of hell would not prevail against them, but to the Church. To the extent, however, that Europe once more becomes a Christendom united in a common faith, she partakes in the promise. Formidable as is the threat which hangs over us, we refuse to despair of the fate of Europe so long as its cause remains linked with that of Redemption. And if the worst should come, we still would not despair. As St. Augustine lay dying in Hippo, he could well have thought that civilization was at an end; yet it was, to the contrary, only beginning. Even if a wave of mud and blood inundates Europe, we believe that what ought to be saved will be saved and men of good will will not be confounded.

IV

*An Author and His Work**

THE last subject that the man of letters whom you honor this evening ought to touch on is, I should say, himself and his work. Yet how can I help thinking of that man and his work, of those poor stories and that simple French writer, who by grace of the Swedish Academy suddenly finds himself all but overcome by an extravagance of honors? No, I do not believe it is vanity that impels me to review the long and winding path that has led me from my obscure childhood to the place I occupy among you tonight.

When I first began to describe the little world of yesteryear that lives again in my books, that small corner of a French province, scarely known even to Frenchmen, where the vacations of my school days were spent, I had no idea that I would attract attention of foreign readers. We are all quite convinced

* Text of the speech delivered in Stockholm, in 1952, on the occasion of Mr. Mauriac's acceptance of the Nobel Prize for literature.

of our utter singularity. We forget that the books which we ourselves found enchanting, those of George Eliot or of Dickens, of Tolstoy or Dostoievski, or of Selma Lagerlof, describe countries very different from our own, people of another race and another religion; and yet we loved them, because we recognized ourselves in them. All humanity is in this or that peasant back home, and all the landscapes in the world coalesce in the horizons familiar to our childish eyes. The novelist's gift is precisely his power to make plain the universal quality concealed in that sheltered world where we were born, and where we first learned to love and suffer.

That mine has appeared so somber to many readers in France and elsewhere, has, I must admit, never ceased to surprise me. Mortal men, by the very fact that they are mortal, dread even the name of death. And so, too, those who have never loved nor been loved, or those who have been forsaken and betrayed, or who have in vain pursued someone beyond their reach, without so much as glancing back at the one who in turn pursued them and whom they did not love—even such people are astonished and dismayed by works of fiction which describe the loneliness of human beings even in the arms of love. "Tell us the things that please us," they say, as the Jews

71

said to the prophet Isaiah, "deceive us with pleasant falsehoods."

Yes, the reader asks to be deceived by pleasant falsehoods. And yet the works that have lived and still live in the memory of man are those that accepted the human drama as a whole, and did not falter before that incurable solitariness in whose bosom each one of us must live and face his destiny until death, that final solitude, since in the end we die alone.

Such is the world as a novelist without hope depicts it. Such is the dismal world into which your great Strindberg transports you. And it would have been my world also, if from the first strivings of conscious life, I had not possessed a great hope. A hope that pierces like a flash of fire the gloom I have described. Black is my color, and people judge me by this, and, for some reason or other, not by the light that penetrates it and burns there secretly. In France every time a wife attempts to poison her husband or strangle her lover, people say to me, "There's a subject for you . . ." I am supposed to have a kind of museum of horrors. I specialize in monsters. And yet, on one essential point my characters differ from almost all of those that populate our present-day fiction: they are aware that they have a soul. In this

post-Nietzschean Europe where the echo of Zarathustra's cry: "God is dead," reverberates still, and
where the fearful results of it have not yet fully run
their course, perhaps all my characters do not believe
in the living God; but they are all aware of that part
of their being which knows evil and which is capable
of not committing it. They know what evil is. They
all feel somehow that they are responsible for their
actions, and that their actions in turn affect the destiny of others.

For my heroes, however worthless they may be, to
live is to participate in an infinite movement, an indefinite surpassing of self. Human beings who do not
doubt that life has a direction and a goal are not
prone to despair. The despair of modern man is born
of his belief in the absurdity of the world—his despair and also similarly his addiction to myths of sub-
stitution. It is, in the last analysis, the sense of the
absurd that makes man inhuman. The day Nietzsche
proclaimed the death of God, he heralded at the same
time the terrible days we have lived through and the
days still to come in which the human person,
emptied of his soul and thus denied a personal destiny, is made into a beast of burden. More abused
than beasts of burden, in fact, by the Nazis and by
those who still employ their methods today; for a

horse, a mule, or an ox at least have cash value, but the human animal, procured without cost thanks to a well devised system of purges, is worth only as much as he can produce—until he collapses.

A writer who focuses his work on human being made in the image of the Father, redeemed by the Son, and illumined by the Holy Spirit could never, possibly, as I see it, be considered a master of despair, no matter how somber a picture he paints.

True, the coloring still remains somber. That is because he sees human nature as wounded, if not corrupted. It stands to reason that the human story as told by a Christian novelist is no idyll, since he is forbidden to shut his eyes to the mystery of evil.

But to be obsessed by evil is also to be obsessed by purity, by childlike goodness. I am sorry that some of my critics, reading too hastily, fail to notice the place that children occupy in my stories. A child's dream is the keystone of all my books: children love and exchange their first kisses, and for the first time experience loneliness—all the things I cherish in the music of Mozart. People see the vipers plainly in my novels but fail to see the dove that nests in many a chapter, because in my works childhood is the lost paradise where the first acquaintance with the mystery of evil is made.

74

The mystery of evil. . . . There are no two ways about it: Either we must deny its existence, or else accept it in all its manifestations within and without, in our personal history and passions as well as in the history of external events, written in human blood by the will to power of empires. I have always been convinced that individual and collective crimes are closely linked; and in my capacity of journalist I have only tried to make clear that the day to day horrors of our political history are no more than the visible consequences of the invisible history unfolding in the secrecy of the human heart.

We who live beneath a sky still streaked with the smoke of crematoriums, have paid a high price to find out that evil is really evil. Before our very eyes we have seen these crematoriums devour millions of innocent people, including children. And the story goes on. The concentration camp system is taking deep root in age-old lands where Christ has been loved, adored, and worshipped for centuries. With terror we watch that portion of the globe where men still enjoy the rights of man, where the human mind is still free, contract before our eyes like the piece of shagreen leather in Balzac's tale.

Do not imagine for a moment that I am blind to the challenge which the existence of evil in the world poses for my faith. In the Christian outlook evil still remains the most agonizing of mysteries. The man who in the midst of the crimes of history perseveres in his faith has still to reckon with the perduring scandal: the seeming uselessness of the Redemption. The reasons given by the theologians for the existence of evil have always left me unpersuaded, reasonable as they are, in fact just because they are so reasonable. The answer that eludes us is not of the order of reason, but of charity. An answer contained wholly and entirely in St. John's words: "God is love." Nothing is impossible to that Living Love, not even to draw all things to itself, and that too, is written.

Forgive me for broaching a problem that in every age has stirred up so many commentaries, disputes, heresies, persecutions, and martyrdoms. But, after all, it is a novelist talking to you, the one you have preferred to all others; so it must be that you attach some value to what has served as his inspiration. Very well, he can assure you that the things he has written in the light of faith and hope does not contradict the experience of his readers who share neither his faith nor his hope. To cite another case, we find that Graham Greene's Christian view of life does not disturb the agnostics among his admirers. Chesterton remarked that whenever something extraordinary occurs in Christianity it is ultimately because something extraordinary in reality corresponds to it. If we were to pursue this point further, we would perchance discover the reason for the mysterious appeal that works of Catholic inspiration, such as those of my friend, Graham Greene, have for the vast dechristianized public which devours his books and delights in his films.

Yes, a vast dechristianized public! As André Malraux has expressed it: "Revolution today plays the role once played by eternal life." But what if the revolution is the myth? And life eternal the unique reality?

Whatever the answer, we all agree on one point: this dechristianized humanity is a humanity crucified. What power on earth can ever destroy the complicity between the suffering of mankind and the Cross? Even your Strindberg, who plumbed the lowest depths from which the psalmist cried out, yes, Strindberg himself expressed the desire, I am told, to have engraved on his tomb a single phrase, a phrase which alone suffices to force the gates of eternity: *Crux ave, spes unica!** He, also, who suffered so much sought repose in the shelter of that hope, and in the shadow

* Hail, oh Cross, our only hope. (Transl.)

77

of that love. And it is in his name that your laureate
begs to be forgiven for these all too personal remarks,
which perhaps struck too serious a note. Yet could he
better repay you for the honors you have heaped
upon him than by opening to you not only his heart
but his soul? And having delivered to you the secret
of his torment through his characters he owed it to
you this evening to let you know the secret of his
peace.

V

*Anguish**

It is not without certain misgivings, and I might say not entirely without anguish, that I find myself last, after so many eminent speakers, to talk to you on anguish. In the first place, I did not have the good fortune of hearing them, so I run the risk of repeating many things they said. Moreover, my topic is one of the foremost themes of contemporary philosophy; and I am the last man in the world who could be called a philosopher; or, if I am, it is without my knowledge and consent. Besides, unlike the philosophers, I am a long way from accepting anguish, or enduring it. But who am I to dispute with them?

What a piece of ill luck for a simple novelist to be born in an age when philosophers rule even in the world of fiction and in the theatre! He does not cut a very intelligent figure speaking as he does in

* A lecture delivered in Geneva on September 10, 1953.

the language of every day; any child who happens by can understand him.

You will be indulgent with me, therefore, if I confess that in preparing this lecture I did not reread Kierkegaard, or the existentialist philosophers of Germany and France. And when I say "reread," you can see I am boasting; you must remember I was born in Gascogny. But take my word for it, in speaking to you on anguish, I prefer to forget what the philosophers have written about it. In treating a subject as hackneyed as this one, I think the best way is for us to suppose that no one had ever discussed it before, and to see what our own souls and long experience have to tell us about anguish, about our own private anguish. This is the anguish which we learn from no one else, and which chokes our heart from the moment we first realize that there is something tragic in the mere fact of being a living man—a man condemned to die who enjoys a reprieve of unknown duration. A reprieve, however, that grows shorter year by year; so that our life is much like the piece of shagreen leather which Balzac's hero watches with terror as it shrinks in his trembling hand until it is hardly bigger than a coin.

Anguish is so much a part of man's estate that it manifests itself from earliest childhood, and how cruelly! If you have the gift of retracing the pathways of your life from its beginnings, if the child you used to be is still a familiar memory, you will recall so vividly as to feel, and live again through, the first terrors of an unlighted room. You can hear the slow, heavy steps on the stairs, as you hide again beneath the sheet. You can feel the hot tears on your cheeks, as from your schoolboy's cot you watch the gas-flame cast flickering shadows on the dormitory wall. Perhaps, you too were a small boy somewhat bullied, who did not feel quite as strong as the others in a school yard full of shouts and quarrelling. Perhaps you quailed at the thought of being called to the blackboard by a scornful teacher so adept at making an idiot of you in front of the whole class.

Perhaps there was also a room in your house where a few months or a few years earlier someone had died, and where the shutters remained closed forever as if upon a horrible mystery. Every object there seemed touched by the dark enchantment of the place: the water glass, the motionless clock, the sunken-in armchair near the fireplace where no fire would ever again be lighted.

Yes, for many a child anguish is a secret and permanent state which could become the onset of madness if it were not for that unstinted tenderness with

81

which his mother showers and caresses him at every moment of the day, and even in the dead of night with all its terrors, when suddenly he feels a cherished hand on his forehead and the gentle breath in his hair, and when he hears the voice softly chiding: "What's the matter, my silly little one? What are you afraid of? I am here. Now close your eyes and go to sleep."

And of what were we afraid? Here is one fact these childhood memories help us to establish: Anguish does not come from outside, and it is in no way bound up with the catastrophes of any particular epoch. Anguished child that I was, I lived at a time when the only war we knew concerned King Behanzin, and when, as the refrain of the blind man in the courtyard of our house reminded us, the French flag had just been planted in Madagascar. People around us argued a great deal about a man named Dreyfus; but his misfortune meant little to us. And all persons of consequence whom I saw, and who personally would not have as much as harmed a fly, feared only one thing: that Dreyfus would not be cashiered and condemned for the second time. My anguish of later years was already alive in this small child of a well-to-do family in a Third Republic that was middle-class, powerful, wealthy, and pacific—though prone to conquest of an uncostly sort.

Of course I do not claim for a moment that the age of disasters which began in 1914, but whose first rumblings could be heard long before, did nothing to foster modern anguish, or that there is no relationship of cause to effect between the woes of our times and the existential anguish of "the being in the world." Nevertheless, even though these events have been tragic enough to cause us to confuse our anguish with the vicissitudes of History, they did not create it. Let us say they would not allow us to be diverted from it—in the sense Pascal used the word —nor to deny it. It is my belief that even in periods of history which present nothing particularly tragic, in peaceful and happy times (peaceful and happy at least for the privileged ones, for there are no happy times for the working class) mankind was no less prey to all the misfortunes that being a man entails; to the sorrows of him who loves and is not loved, who is loved but cannot love in return, who has had a son and lost him, who was young and is young no longer, who has been strong and virile and one day hears the doctor say after a prolonged examination, "Perhaps an operation might help. . . ," and who hears the automobiles in the street, a radio on the floor below, a woman's laughter, knowing withal that in six months he will be dead.

And even if he is spared such trials there is still ahead what Michelet told us is torture enough: old age, with its failure of one function after another, the decline of the mind, the gradual and stealthy approach of inevitable dissolution.

At the outset, I agreed to proffer nothing on this subject except what grew out of my personal experience. Right here, therefore, I am obliged to part company with Michelet and many others. This is the fork in the road, and after having talked to you in such depressing tones I would now exclaim, as Father Lacordaire once did to his congregation at Nancy, "My brothers, I bring you happiness."

But it was a sermon that began like that, and I shudder at the thought that this too is a sermon, which a simple layman like myself ventures to deliver before you. What a paradox, when I think of how little attention I pay to my own pastor's sermons. However, we are all like that: we preach to others, but do not care to be preached to ourselves. One day, Paul Claudel, who had just endured a homily, said to me, "It is really incredible, you know, that Christianity was spread by preaching." But what else did he himself do all his life, our beloved and great Claudel, but spread the word of God? And what is there for any of us to do in this world—as many as we may be—if we belong to Christ?

So you must pardon me if I make bold to use Father Lacordaire's words and say, "I bring you happiness." I am well aware that a large number of my listeners this evening are not Christians in belief. But even they do not look for anything but a Christian talk from me, I feel sure. They would be astonished, indeed scandalized, if for reasons of expediency, I refrained from giving voice to what in my view is the only happiness, the one happiness that has not disappointed or betrayed me. I bring you happiness, the kind of happiness a Christian begins to discover at my age. The fact is that as I have grown older, age has relaxed its grip. "As a man grows older he becomes more conscious of eternal things," Romano Guardini has written, "He becomes less restive, so that the voices coming from beyond can be heard more clearly. As eternity closes in, the reality of time begins to fade." I remember a prayer of St. Gertrude, who must have been very old when she recited it, in which she calls Christ, "Love of the evening of my life," and invokes Him in words that I find so beautiful: "Oh, my Jesus of eventide, give me rest in tranquil sleep." But all this was already expressed at the very dawn of the Christian era, when the aged Simeon embraced the infant God: *"Nunc dimittis servum tuum, Domine . . ."** René Bazin never penned a finer line than the one I read on his tombstone: "When age overtakes us, all things forsake us, but God comes."

He does not come as a defense which we conjure up against anguish. On the contrary, it was throughout our stormy youth when anguish was our permanent state that we would not turn to Him, that we kept aloof from Him. No, it is not our anguish that creates God, rather it is the peace and quiet which comes in the wake of a waning life and enables us at last to pay attention to the Response that has been offered us without cease throughout the whole of our troubled life. But we preferred to remain in our suffering, because we preferred to cling to our sin. What more do I know today than I knew as the desperate adolescent I was then? Actually, it was not knowledge I lacked, but a love of happiness, a love of peace. How long it takes to learn how to love. Since the days of old Lucretius, it has been taken for granted that fear is the creator of the gods; and in one form or an-

---

* "Now thou dost dismiss thy servant in peace, O Lord. . . ." (Transl.)

other the philsophers have gone on reviving this old theme, which can be found today again at the core of the Nietzschean and Marxist offensive against faith in the Infinite Being. I told you at the start that you should expect nothing from me on the subject anguish that is not taken from my own personal experience. Well, my experience shows that far from fearing anguish I loved it, preferred it to God Himself. So little, in fact, did it prompt me to create an imaginary God to gain relief from it, that, contrariwise, I sought reasons and excuses to flee from that loving Presence within and around me, to which I preferred the sadness that is born of lust.

No, it is not anguish that creates the Father in heaven whom Christ taught us to know and love. Quite the reverse, it is that melancholy pleasure of our never ending youth—yes, never ending, because the heart stays young long after youth has departed. It is this dark enchantment with anguish which disposes us to turn away from God and even deny that He exists, and which supplies us with proofs and arguments against His goodness and against His love.

Doubtless you will object that this is not true of all men, but only of writers and poets, who prize their anguish as the very source of their inspiration, and very particularly that form of anguish which is the fruit of the combat between a desire for God and the flesh. Yes, perhaps . . . I have often quoted and applied to myself Maurice de Guerin's figure of speech which compares his thought to a heavenly fire burning on the horizon between two worlds. It is this distress of a person torn by the choice between God and the world, which is in fact at the root of many artists' struggle and which is at once the source of their torment and their delights.

"If thou didst know the gift of God. . . ." said Christ to the woman of Samaria. And what is the gift of God? The very opposite of anguish. "I leave you peace, my peace I give you," said Our Lord to his friends on that last night before entering his agony. This peace is precisely what we do not want, and it fills us with dread, because, I repeat, we do not love peace. "Rise up, O tempest of our desire!" This cry of René at the dawn of the romantic era reveals the vocation of unhappiness that many of our young folk have chosen. The poets of despair were the ones to whom we first turned, and it was the eternal sadness in the prince of darkness that first attracted us. A literary pose? Yes, of course—but a strange sort of posturing, this despair which in surrealist circles has so often been authenticated by suicide. St. John denounces it, this hatred of peace, in the first lines of

88

his Gospel: he tells us that the light came into the world and men refused it, because they preferred darkness. A man seeks the shadows in order to indulge himself and not be seen. The victory of Christ in his life is the difficult acceptance of peace in the light.

I understand very well the objection you all must have in mind: Christianity itself is an anguish, and indeed it is not enough merely to say that a Christian anguish exists. All critics of Christianity of the nineteenth century accused it of being contrary to Nature, of casting a shroud over the world, of maligning life. What is the answer to these charges? Is their truth so overwhelmingly apparent?

I make no attempt to dodge the issue. Christianity is a word that has covered many conflicting tendencies, which have found Christians themselves at loggerheads. With the result that those who were called to love one another have gone so far as to burn one another at the stake. . . . One of these tendencies—that of St. Augustine, of Calvin, of Jansenius—was conceived in a spirit of fear and trembling, of anguish in its harshest sense. For there is also an anguish that is sweet, the anguish of love, which consists wholly in the regret at having offended the loved one, in the fear of being no longer loved, or of no longer feeling love ourselves. The love of the creature for the Creator is no more immune than any other human affection from what Marcel Proust calls the intermittencies of the human heart. But you understand very well that it is not this kind of distress that we mean when we speak of fear and trembling.

I told you before that I am not a philosopher. Neither am I a theologian, and I ask the pardon of any theologians who may be listening to me this evening if I venture on their terrain. They can be sure, my steps thereon will be few indeed. Let it suffice for me to remind you that the Christian anguish which Nietzsche denounced stemmed wholly and entirely from the Jansenist obsession with individual salvation.

And when I say "Jansenist," I am not unmindful that I am speaking in the city of Calvin; it is simply that for a French Catholic, it is easier to talk of Jansenism than of Calvinism—the more so because (and I am reluctant to tell you this) Port Royal was my parish. I hasten to add, however, that the Jansenist doctrine of grace has never found a place among my beliefs, and that Mr. de Saint-Cyran has always impressed me as a theologian of the most sinister make. Let us say, in any case, that in France, not to mention any other country, Port Royal remains the principal source of that anguish which is rooted in the obsession of personal salvation.

In accord with an unforeseeable design, the Infinite Being imparts or denies His grace to His creatures stained from the moment of birth, totally impotent in all save evil, but where evil is concerned as potent as a god. Thus we are consigned naked, trembling, and defenseless into the hands of this arbitrary infinite being. Such is the provenance of this anguish.

Never fear, I do not claim to be able to settle in a few words this evening a question that has engaged the best efforts of a whole line of Christian thinkers through the centuries—especially as I would be unable, for instance, to tell you just where Pascal differs with Luther and Calvin and with the doctrine of justification by faith alone. I can only point to you that permanent wellspring of anguish and even of despair, which a certain type of theology causes to gush from the heart pierced by its lance. This doctrine has bred that numberless and pitiable family, that scourge of Catholic confessors, the scrupulous: men and women alike, obsessed by trifles, adorers of a meddling divinity who must be approached by all sorts of ruses. I believe it was the very irreverent

André Gide who used to lampoon Catholics for their "salvation cramps." Cramps so painful that many young men who began by following Christ left Him in order to escape from the scruple, the obsession of having to render an accounting of the least thought, their slightest desire. They ended by casting their entire Christian heritage overboard. "The marvelous thing about Communism," one of these youngsters, turned Marxist, told me one day, "is that my personal salvation no longer interests me."

Well now, what I want to suggest to you as a defense against that form of anguish, is another anguish: an anguish that generates peace and joy. What I prescribe is a sort of spiritual homeopathy, the cure of anguish by means of anguish.

The obsession with personal salvation will never be mastered and overcome until the problem is transposed onto the level of charity. Not, of course, that we should cease to cherish the hope of salvation, nor that the whole life of a Christian should not tend towards eternal life and the possession of its Love, which is Christ. A passionate desire for salvation, yes —but not a fixation, not an obsession in the pathological sense of the term. In my youth many of us were charmed by the words Pascal puts into the mouth of

Christ: "I was thinking of you in my agony. I shed this particular drop of blood for you." May I confess that they charm me much less today, because I detect in this desire for a drop of blood shed for ourselves in particular the satisfaction of one who is prepared to consign the most of the human race to eternal reprobation, and who is not at all distressed by the thought of being set apart in a little flock of the elect.

Anguish transmuted into charity, anguish for others, frees us from the fear aroused in so many souls by the mystery of predestination. It frees us from that preoccupation with personal salvation— not so far as it is good and necessary, but so far as it is morbid. Now our anguish no longer concerns ourselves alone; it encompasses humanity, or at least that portion of it which we regard as "our neighbor," and which may include a whole social class, or even an entire race. For a priest-worker or for one of our pastors of a poor parish, the entire working class is his neighbor. Just as for so many of us the neighbor was the entire Jewish race in the days of the Nazi persecution—and at the moment I have occasion to know from personal experience how far the devotion and love we feel for a persecuted race can go.

For some of our contemporaries hell consists of other people; but for us, others are Christ. He told us

93

Himself that the Son of Man came to seek and to save those who were lost—yes, all who were lost, not merely this or that person for whom He had particularly consecrated one scant drop of blood.

Surely, I would be an odd sort of Christian if I did not believe that the Christian life means first and foremost a personal relationship with God for each one of us; if I did not believe the words: "You have not chosen me, but I have chosen you"; if I did not understand what Newman meant by "My Creator and I." It stands to reason that extension of our anguish to the measure of suffering humanity will only bring forth its full fruits if our apostolate is rooted in a close intimacy with Christ. It is, and always has been, my belief that the Christian life is essentially a friendship, a love, in other words, the most personal and most individual part of us. I have always believed that every one of us has been called by name. Preceding every conversion there is always the meeting at the crossroads of which Father Lacordaire speaks: that adorable Being, demanding, refusing to let us go, Whom nothing discourages, to Whom we prefer so many creatures that forsake us or whom we forsake. But He is there, always there, and indeed, never so near as when we think He is far away, awaiting His hour, which for so many souls, alas, is their last hour, when all further chance of betrayal is gone.

What did our Love do, what did this Christ do, Whom every faithful soul strives to imitate, but take all human anguish upon Himself? We, therefore, should also shoulder our share of it. The saints did so literally, to the point of identifying themselves really with the Son forsaken by the Father in the horror of night. Bernanos penetrated deeply into the secret of that holy agony. And it is this which endows his priestly characters, especially his country curé, with a mysterious dimension. For us, simple members of the Faith, it is enough to be one with our brothers in their anguish, as Our Lord Himself experienced it.

It seems to me that it is to the credit of the Church today that they have a better understanding of all this than the generations preceding us. The Church in France especially offers admirable examples in this regard, some of which are well known, such as the *Mission de Paris* and the priest-workers. Then there are the Dominican Friars who have entered the active apostolate and the new Orders of Little Brothers and Little Sisters of Father de Foucauld, both cleric and lay, who in factories, fishing boats, and on the docks, in the leprosariums, and in the *medinas* of the Orient put into practice the vow of absolute poverty, which Father de Foucauld was unable to obtain from any one while he lived; it is our generation, thirty years after his death, that will answer his call.

That, ladies and gentlemen, is the curious remedy for anguish which I prescribe—peace and joy that are the offspring of our anguish: "Peace I leave with you, my peace I give unto you: not as the world giveth, do I give unto you." We now understand the profound meaning of this last promise made by the Son of Man before entering upon His agony. At the summit of anguish this peace and joy is to be found, which consists in uniting ourselves—each according to his vocation—to the suffering of the hungry, the persecuted, the imprisoned, the tortured, the exploited. Such is the Christian paradox.

As I near the end of my talk, there is one thing that disturbs me. The fear that you might get the impression that to my mind the great portion of humanity which lives outside the pale of Christian hope is by the same token doomed to despair. No, most assuredly, I do not believe this. But I served you notice at the outset that I would reveal to you my own personal defense against anguish, the only one I know. I am not blind to the fact that innumerable human beings follow other paths. The fact that they put their whole faith in the earth does not deter them from working with all their might hopefully and joyfully for the dawn of a new humanity.

Where they are concerned, however, I want to correct what I said at the beginning of this talk to the effect that the events and catastrophes of history have no real influences on human anguish. On second thought, I would say that is not true for people who pin all their hopes on the "progress of lights"—as they used to say in the eighteenth century —in the future of science, and in the advent of social justice. How can anyone deny that human hope as it existed in France in 1789, and later at the outset of the industrial era, has suffered setbacks of the bloodiest kind and has continued to suffer them since 1914 and as we advance into the atomic age? We know the price that had to be paid for man's mastery over matter and his acquisition of its most secret laws. In this connection, we have only to mention Hiroshima; the mere word tells the story, and always will.

The same thing is true of the Communist revolution, which on a significant part of our planet is already an accomplished fact, and has a long history behind it. You will understand why I do not wish to develop my thought on this subject here. I have said enough, however, for you to understand that human anguish is linked to the events of history insofar as these events destroy the object itself of our hope. The atomic bomb in the field of scientific research and the concentration camp in the field of social revolution are cause enough, I should say, to unsettle the faith of those who have believed passionately and exclusively in human progress.

We Christians know that earth-bound expectations and hope are not the same thing, that it is possible to have lost all hope for the temporal salvation of mankind and still await the Kingdom of God. We await it confidently, even in the era of the atomic bomb and the concentration camp. I hasten to add, however, that our hope is not concerned with eternity alone; it is also concerned with the grim world of the living. For whatever crimes the will to power may lead to in visible history, they cannot prevent the leaven of which Christ speaks from doing its work, ceaselessly, in the human masses. The fire He came to cast on the earth burns quietly and without fail beneath the surface; and the most bloody years of history are none the less years of grace.

"Thy kingdom come." We ask it in the *Pater,* and

98

for nearly two thousand years since this prayer was first taught to us millions upon millions have uttered it in the absolute certainty of one day being heard. But we have already been heard, the Kingdom has already come. It is within us. So that we are never defeated save in appearance; and since our anguish is the very condition of our peace, our defeat is the very condition of our victory. "Have confidence, I have overcome the world." He who threw this challenge to the world did so at the very hour when he was about to be betrayed, outraged, mocked, and nailed to the gibbet of slaves.

St. Paul tells us that all of creation groans and suffers the pangs of parturition. Our anguish is like labor-pains which to the ephemeral creatures that we are seem interminable. Still we know, we who have kept the faith, what the outcome will be. To such of our contemporaries as have succumbed to anguish and may be about to lose heart, the only consolation we can offer is what St. Paul said to the faithful of Rome: "Who shall separate us from the love of Christ? Shall tribulation? or distress? or persecution? or danger? or the sword? But in all these things we overcome, because of him who has loved us."

By what right or what authority do you say this! I

feel I must ask myself this one last time, for I have a very strong feeling that I am being impertinent, not to say shameless. Moreover, I have had qualms about a letter which I found at the desk of my hotel the evening I arrived. It was from a young Swiss who expressed indignation that I would dare to appear on this platform, I who am, you are to understand, one of the main persons responsible for modern anguish.

Undoubtedly, this Genevan youth rates me too highly. If I had never written at all, I do not believe that human anguish would on that account have been alleviated in the slightest degree. But, after all, it is quite true: every writer, every creative artist is a fomenter of trouble. He demoralizes in the very lofty sense that André Gide said he wished to be a demoralizing influence; that is, by forcing man to see and know himself as he really is, not as he would like to appear; in short, by compelling him to drop the pose.

Shall I confess something to you? The older I get the less I experience any scruple for having offended in this way. For the sad thing, after all—we can probably agree on this point at the end of our talk—is not that so many people feel anguish, but on the contrary, that they do not. Or that they feel anguish only for themselves, and that assaults against the human personality, of which they have been eye-witnesses and too often accomplices, do not disturb them in their tranquil possession of privileges or in the exercise of their will to power.

If there is an anguish which ought to be conquered and overcome, there is another which is the manifestation of the spirit in us, its very breath. This is the good anguish, of which there must be no cure. No, under no circumstances must it be cured, because it is a sign that the soul is alive within you, that soul which has been entrusted to you and from which an accounting will be asked for the portion of human anguish that God knows it ought to have assumed. That is the meaning of the terrible words of St. John of the Cross: "On the last day, you will be judged on love."

VI

*The Living God**

WHEN we pronounce the name of God, what thoughts does it arouse? In all the years we have spoken of Him, who have we meant by God? Who was He, when as children we first began to pray to Him and perhaps to love Him? "I know whom I have believed," St. Paul declared to Timothy. But, truly, do we know in Whom we believe? It would be a mistake to think that the desire to be sincere is all we need to give a clear reply to this question. I am asking you as I would ask God if I were alone, and with the same determination that I would then have to say nothing but the truth. Here, however, we are not in the comforting realm of clear and distinct ideas. Moreover, short as the span of human life is, it is very possible that the child, the adolescent, the young man, the adult, and the aged, while invoking

* Text of a lecture delivered at the closing session of the Conference of Catholic Intellectuals of November 1953.

102

the same name, have perhaps not invoked the same Being.

In my own case, at a very early age God was the same for me as He is today; very early I pursued Him or fled from Him along the same paths on which I still run breathlessly today. Oh, without a doubt, when I was a child, God must have seemed to me as Francis Jammes describes Him:

> *I believed that God was*
> *An old man with snow-white hair,*
> *Who always gave you what you asked Him for.*

But did I really believe this? I suppose I did. And yet, for as long as I can remember, it seems to me that my thoughts did not rise by themselves toward the Infinite Being. I recall how in Bible History the very name of God seemed vaguely suspect to me, because the God of the Jews was nothing like the One I knew and loved. Did I know Him, then? And love Him? Yes, of course, and though I cannot say with certainty when it was, I believe that the Incarnation was my starting point, that He first entered my life as the God Incarnate. I cannot possibly imagine how the mere child that I was could have come upon the living God except through Christ. It was, no doubt, because there was someone like myself, with a body like my own, whose heart of flesh was prone to love and to suffer like mine, someone who as a child was crucified in His crib long before He was on His Cross, someone I knew and could talk with in secret at any time; it was because one day Christ taught me to say, "Our Father Who art in heaven," that I knew and believed that heaven is where our Father is. Because at every moment of his earthly life Christ repeated "My Father," I knew the Being beyond all imagining to be a living person.

Very early in life, apparently, I was unusually attentive to the words of Our Lord, especially in St. John, where the Second Person of the Blessed Trinity gives testimony to the First. For me, Jesus Christ was a witness of the eternally living Godhead as the apostles were witnesses of Christ, living, dead, buried, and risen. But Our Lord does not only use the words "My Father" or "Our Father." He also says *"The* Father": "The hour is coming, and is now here, when the true worshippers will worship *the* Father in spirit and in truth. For *the* Father also seeks such to worship Him." Here the simple indefinite article, more effectively than the possessive pronoun, brings home to us that infinite paternity which has been, is, and always will be concerned with the life and death of every person; that paternity which embraces all of us, from Adam to the last man, as mysterious as Adam, who on the last day will draw the last human breath.

Here for me, Christ again intervenes directly. It is He who inclines my mind to grasp the mystery of this myriad paternity. It is the mystery of the Eucharist, that total gift of Our Lord to each faithful member of the flock who communicates each morning throughout the world, almost as if there were no one else in the world but we who receive Him and He who gives Himself to us, that mystery which we have used and perhaps abused for so many years, that intimate and habitual contact—yes, I say it is this mystery that introduces us to the idea of the Father Who gives Himself wholly to every single human being. If you asked me which words of Our Lord carry the greatest assurance as to the inscrutable Fatherhood of the Infinite Being, mystery of transcendence swallowed up, as it were, in the contingent world of every day, I would remind you of the ineffable verse which no doubt you all know by heart—that promise which the faithful Christian never ceases to meditate upon, and whose fulfillment he can verify within himself, if he keeps himself the least bit clean. It is the 23rd verse of the fourteenth chapter of St. John: "If anyone love me, he will keep my word, and my Father will love him, and we will come and make our abode with him."

I realize how suspect is any mention of experience of experimentation in these matters. Nevertheless, how can we fail to recognize that this promise applies not only to saints but also to sinners; I mean to those who repent, struggle, and strive to remain faithful.

I have no doubt that there are many people who have attained to the living God mostly by using the reason God gave them, and that they first saw the light through their intellect and understood before feeling drawn. But, whenever one of them treats me with a sort of affectionate disdain, as sometimes happens, I take comfort in repeating to myself those words which will not pass away: "No one cometh to the Father but by me." And again, "I am the door of the sheep . . . I am the door. If any man enter by me he shall be safe."

Though I cannot say exactly when, I believe it was in very early childhood, probably about the time of my First Communion that these words of Our Lord which speak of the Father, My Father, and Our Father, Whom we approach only through Christ, introduced me to the living God. But as soon as I began to search for an intellectual justification of my faith—when I reached the age at which even the least philosophically-minded awaken to the world of ideas—it was my discovery of Pascal between my fifteenth and seventeenth years that made me fully conscious of what I had vaguely experienced. Thanks to him, I became imbued by a train of thought from which I have never since departed. I realized that I belonged to a particular spiritual family which though very large was always a bit suspect. Need I remind you here that when Pascal wrote: "It is the heart that senses God, not reason. That is what faith is: God grasped through the heart, not through reason. . . ," in referring to the heart he did not mean some sort of perception by the senses, or gushing of feeling. To him, knowledge by means of the heart was the intuitive grasp of first principles. It is not the intelligence which comprehends, said he, but the heart which senses "that there are three dimensions in space, and that numbers are infinite."

This God of Pascal's, reached intuitively, is not, moreover, God the First Cause or God the Prime Mover, Who in the beginning imparted the initial impulse which sent the universe on its way. Nor is He God, the Lawmaker, the hair-splitting Judge, Who rewards and punishes the trembling human flock. The first words written on the piece of paper which Pascal wore stitched in the lining of his coat tell us all we need to know: "God of Abraham, God of Isaac, God of Jacob, not of the philosophers and scholars." They summarize the fragment from the *Pensées* with which doubtless you are familiar, but you will forgive me if I repeat it at length here again. In dealing with a subject which, I dare say, overwhelms us—even though we may be bursting with it, and even though it includes what we hold dearest and for which even the weakest and most cowardly of us would, with the help of grace, give his life—can we do better than go over in our hearts words which have been and always will be a revelation for us? Furthermore, it seems to me that the essence of the mystery upon which all your thoughts have been centered during the current week is fully expressed by it: "The God of Christians is not a God Who is simply the Author of geometric verities and of the order of the elements; that is the view of pagans and Epicureans. He is not merely a God Who exercises His Providence over the lives and fortunes of men, to bestow a happy span of years on those who adore Him; such is the portion of the Jews. But the God of Abraham, Isaac and Jacob, the God of the Christians, is a God of love and consolation: a God Who fills the souls and bodies of those He possesses, a God Who makes them conscious of their inner wretchedness and of His Infinite Mercy, Who becomes one with them in their inmost soul, Who fills it with humility, joy, confidence, and love; Who makes them incapable of any other goal than Himself."

Such is the living God. And still, Pascal did not tell all. Perhaps like all the men of Port Royal and members of their spiritual family, he was excessively concerned, even obsessed with the problem of individual salvation. And as for the drop of blood shed particularly for us—I am not so sure today as I was in my youth that it is good to dwell thereupon too complacently. We are not members of a small trembling band of the elect cut off from the reprobate hordes of humanity. The Son of Man came to seek and to save that which was lost. He told us so Himself. The living God, revealed to us by the Son as the Father, as our Father, is known to us by another name, which defines Him in His very essence —a name written everywhere in the Gospels, underlying everything the Son said of the Father, but which it was given to St. John to confide to us on two occasions in his first Epistle: "God is love." It is not we who have loved God, but He Who has loved us. The living God is living Love.

Ask the true lovers of God—a St. Francis of Assisi, a St. Vincent de Paul—what are the implications of this thrilling truth. Or in today's dark world, ask our clergy in poverty-stricken parishes (and what parish has no poor?), the Little Brothers of Father de Foucauld, or many religious in every Order; ask any Sister who works with the poor, whatever the make of her head-dress or the color of her veil. But also ask that so many of the faithful of today, our unknown saints of the lay apostolate or of the apostolate to the workers. If the living God is a living Love, a Christian cannot help but imitate this living Love.

How far should our imitation go? No one can say with certainty where that duty ends, nowadays especially when our neighbor can no longer be limited to this or that poor soul whom we aid by almsgiving or whose wounds we dress. For our parochial clergy who minister to the workers, the neighbor happens to be the entire laboring class, just as during the Nazi persecutions it was the whole Jewish people.

And today also our neighbor means those dark skinned races, whom we have made our protegés— and by methods that were not always gentle, to say the very least. Yes, they are our nearest neighbor, if we pretend at all to be worshippers of the God of Abraham, Isaac, and Jacob, who is also the God of Ishmael. It takes many years to acquire the courage to face so simple a truth. As a rule, we are well along in years and almost ready to embark on our last journey, before the scales fall from our eyes. Then at last we see the sophistry and equivocation behind the attempt to maintain a balance between the will to power of a nation, the financial interests of a few men, and the command given us from the beginning to proclaim the Lord to every people and to baptize them in the name of the Father, the Son and the Holy Ghost.

But have no fear, I am not unmindful that I have raised an extremely complex issue here. And, you can be sure, I do not mean to decry whatever is fecund and heroic in the accomplishments of France overseas. No, I do not intend to tread further on this ground, which I have reason enough to know is a sorely debated one. Yet how can one speak of the living God without speaking of living idols? We have come a long way from the Baals and Astartes that Israel worshipped on the heights to our own Astartes and Baals. It is no longer a matter of statues, whether of wood, ivory, or gold. The gods we fashion are nobler, so noble indeed that there is no sacrifice —I mean human sacrifice—which we would deem too great to make to them.

Many martyrs of the first centuries died for refusing to accept the cult of Caesar. But Caesar in our day exacts infinitely more than a cult. In the countries we call totalitarian, he is not satisfied with merely external homage. The gift he wants is that of the whole person, the surrender of one's most secret thoughts. The cult of the Roman Caesars at least did not entail the denial of the Infinite Being; but we have learned how far the demands of the bloody idols of State and Party can go today.

But here is the mystery: We denounce the idols of peoples behind the iron curtain, but are blind to those we worship ourselves. And what a strange capacity for deifying things the men of our country have, even when they are Christians! Actually, what have we not deified, all of us without exception? Money, of course, first of all, science and technology, the social order, the party, the working class, a particular philosophy, a theological system. . . . These we have placed above all question, all criticism, and all judgment.

It is not easy for us to detect this idolatrous element within us, we are so seldom conscious of it. Christians who give way to passions of the heart have no trouble agreeing that the love of a creature is enough to obscure God for them. And this is still more clearly understood by individuals whose lives have been brutally simplified by a dominant vice. But it is much harder for us to conceive how a political, an ideological, or an esthetical passion can separate us from the living God.

"Dear children, guard yourselves from idols." For a long time this last verse of the first Epistle of St. John seemed to hold little significance for us moderns, since it applied to the first Christians in open combat with naked paganism. "Dear children, guard yourselves from idols." Today we realize that we are the little children who must be guarded from idols. It was to us across the centuries that this plea was addressed, to us who walk through a forest of idols. A forest of idols separates us from the living God.

Have we ever got through to this God? Is there any hope of doing so? We realize how utterly presumptuous it would be on our part to answer yes—we who know the price the saints had to pay to possess the living God—we who perhaps have not taken a single step along the route followed by a John of the Cross. Still, as you know, there are humbler paths along which so many poor women, so many mothers of families have advanced toward God without realizing it.

Occasionally at morning Mass, we notice a housewife, with a worn countenance, who slips furtively into her pew. We hear the rattling of her grocery bag as she puts it on the seat, and then we watch her enter into peace. No doubt we would spend our time better if instead of watching others pray we prayed ourselves. Yet this distraction, if it really is one, helps us to realize that these things are possibly simpler than we imagined. "Be ye perfect as your heavenly Father is perfect." This command was not given to a few, it applies to all of us. There is a kind of perfection that is within our reach, within the reach of anyone who loves God. Yes, within the reach of plain and simple people, though perhaps not of us, the intellectuals, as we describe ourselves on the notices of this Convention—not without some pride.

Well, as the poor housewife lays aside her bag of groceries and bottle of milk, let us put aside our little bundle of ready-made ideas and parrotted systems, and let us open our souls to that love whose witnesses we are in the world. A Catholic intellectual, being a writer and a speaker, is essentially that, a witness. And this is our only excuse, it seems to me, for claiming to have something to teach others, and to have the right to speak and be listened to while others hold their peace.

The testimony that is asked of us is not simply

a matter of crying, "Lord, Lord!" in the public square. Every gesture we make, on every occasion, should testify that we are striving to judge human conflict in the light of the God of truth; you understand, of course, that by human conflict I refer to political conflict. Alas, all is clear and simple as long as it is a question of the drama within us, of this poor heart of ours whose twisting and turning, whose wretchedness we know so well. There is scarcely a problem of conscience affecting our personal life that will not give in to a few moments of meditation and prayer. But nothing is clear, nothing is simple when we turn to the problems evoked by history in this sad world or by our conduct as citizens. Since politics are essentially impure, it arouses us to passions which, if not always base, often proceed from the spirit of anger.

How difficult it is for a writer engaged in political affairs to know what the Father expects of him, and the Son, who is meek and humble of heart, and the Holy Virgin, who weeps in front of children and speaks only to young Bernadette! And yet, it was this same Jesus so meek and humble of heart who rent the air with the whip intended for the unworthy money-changers. And it was the maledictions which he heaped upon the Pharisees that aroused their first desire to kill Him in their hearts. And Mary, too, the young maid of Nazareth, exulting at what was being accomplished in her, exclaimed, and will always exclaim in the voices of all the generations which continue to intone her *Magnificat:* "He hath shown might in His arm; He hath scattered the proud in the conceit of their heart. He hath put down the mighty from their seat and hath exalted the humble. He hath filled the hungry with good things and the rich He hath sent empty away." This is much stronger than anything I would dare to write in an editorial.*

You understand, I trust, what my purpose is in quoting these sublime verses, and that it is not to distort their eternal meaning. But do not hope to find justification in the life of Our Lord or of the Holy Virgin and the saints for your own indifference to the world, and its visible history. For the witness of the living God there can be no question about being committed; he cannot help but be a man of action—though there are as many types of action as there are individual vocations. One thing is certain: the Catholic intellectual is called to bear witness both in season and out of season.

Since the intellectual is also a man with passions,

* Mr. Mauriac is literary editor of the French daily, *Le Figaro.*

however, and sometimes holds intense political preferences, he must never lose sight of what God demands of him: that his testimony remain pure. Yes, we ought to hunger and thirst for justice, to be sure, but not hunger and thirst for vengeance. To suffer persecution for justice sake, yes, but not to persecute in the name of justice. The pleasure of besting an opponent, of dominating, of being the stronger; irritation, anger, scorn, if not the hatred, —all these, the witness of the living God must thwart and control within himself, if he does not wish merely to serve, in the name of God whom he claims to love, an ideology made into his idol.

You will wonder, no doubt, whether it is possible in the heat of the battle of ideas, which, unfortunately, is also and above all a battle of human interests, to behave like angels. It was the secret of the saints to act invisibly and powerfully on their environment without a loss of saintliness. But their secret is within our grasp and can be expressed in one brief sentence: contemplation purifies action. Our generation understands this, in my opinion, better than the ones preceding us. Christian sanctity no longer sets up Martha against Mary. The workaday life of a Little Brother or Sister of Jesus is, in reality, a contemplative life. Among the Daughters

of St. Vincent de Paul, among the Little Sisters of
the Poor or of the Assumption, how many there are
who never for an instant lose their sense of the
presence of God!

Contemplation purifies action. So why not political action as well? Indeed, the experience we have
had with Christians in power for the last ten years
inspires thoughts you will allow me to keep to myself; you must admit that in their case mysticism
and politics have made strange bedfellows. But who
are we to cast the stone at them, knowing as we do
the paradoxes that plague a Christian involved in
public affairs? At any rate, believe me, the same
remedy that is valid for the saint is valid for us
journalists and writers. And I do not refer solely to
the saints on our calendars but to the housewife at
early Mass who places her groceries beside her each
morning and enters into peace with her Lord. The
remedy lies in the hidden life of the Father and the
Son abiding in those who love Them, according to
the promise made to us. It is within each one of us
that the true battle is waged. If we win it, the errors,
the setbacks, and even the grave faults of our public
life will not prevent our rejoicing when the hour
comes for us to rest. For we shall have attained and
possessed, here on earth, the Kingdom of God and
His justice.